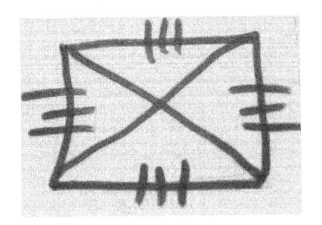

Acknowledgments

Cover Design: Xochipala Maes Valdez

Front Cover Photo: Photographed by Dianne Elkins Jenett.
                     Kali at the Udaygiri Caves in Orissa, 2003.
                     Some scholars date these Jaina caves from
                     100 BCE. One of the oldest goddess images
                     in India and originally from the Jaina
                     tradition, this image is now worshipped as
                     Kali.

Book Design
and Layout: Xochipala Maes Valdez,
                     Three Seeds Design

First Printing May 2007—Napa, California
Second expanded edition published July 2009 – Napa, California
© All Rights Reserved – 2009
The Lilith Institute
http://www.lilithinstitute.com

ISBN 978-0-615-30737-4

Talking to Goddess

Blessings, Invocations, Prayers, Chants, Oriki and Discussions With Spirit

gathered by

D'vorah J. Grenn, Ph.D., Editor

The Lilith Institute
Napa and San Mateo, California

Other works by the author:

Lilith's Fire: Reclaiming our Sacred Lifeforce
(Deborah Grenn-Scott, 2000)

For She Is A Tree of Life: Shared Roots Connecting Women to Deity—
An Organic Theological Inquiry Into Identities, Beliefs And Practices
Among South African Lemba And European-American Jewish Women,
California Institute of Integral Studies doctoral dissertation, 2003,
Accession #AAT 3078795; under Deborah Grenn-Scott. Available through
http:// www.proquest.com/en-US/

"How Women Construct And Are Formed By Spirit: She Who Is
Everywhere In Women's Voices, Kol Isha, Maipfi A Vhafumakadzi" in
She Is Everywhere, Vol. I (Lucia Chiavola Birnbaum, ed.; Authors Choice Press,
2005)

"Connecting With Deity Through a Feminist Metaformic Thealogy"
in Metaformia: A Journal of Menstruation and Culture
Spring 2005 – www.metaformia.org

"Creator Woman—Deity, Snake and Life-Giving Waters: The Active
Female Principle in the Fertile Crescent, Carthage and South Africa" in
She Is Everywhere! Volume II (Annette Wiliams, Karen Villanueva, Lucia
Chiavola Birnbaum, editors; Authors Choice Press, 2008)

"Lilith's Fire: Examining Original Sources of Power, Re-defining Sacred
Texts as Transformative Theological Practice" in Feminist Theology
journal, September 2007

"Claiming The Title Kohenet: Examining Goddess Judaism and the Role
of the Priestess" in Women in Judaism Multidisciplinary Journal, 2008

Dedicated to the girls becoming women...
and the boys becoming men.

May they find non-violent solutions to problems,
And give themselves and each other permission
to respect compassion as much as they do anger.

With reverence & thanks to the ancestors, and to my elders, who have inspired and encouraged me to do this work every step of the way – even when I wasn't listening

Mojuba, love and respect to those of blessed memory who have influenced and guided me, who continue to help me envision and manifest my hopes and dreams from the realms they now inhabit.
I personally thank and name:

Rita Rosalind Kolb Grenn and Verena Rosmarie LaMar-Grenn
Anna Bernstein Kolb and David Kolb, Esther, Thelma and Leo Kolb
Gertrud Silberstein Gruenbaum, Julius Gruenbaum
My great-grandmothers Bernstein & Silberstein
My great-grandfathers Kolb and Gruenbaum
Hanna Gruenbaum Eule Minkin
Franziska Silberstein
Dr. Mildred Sabath
Bernice Rifas
Eleanor Kolb
Grete Levy
Trude Rau
Julian Eule
Regina Possony
Rabbi Sanford Rosen
Professor Matshaya Mathivha
Masotsha Mathivha
Anica Vesel Mander
Gen Lawler
Pam Lawler
Vroni Gfeller
Asphodel Long
Savina Teubal
Monica Sjoo
Mamie Scott
"Mom Pearl" Scott

Moyuba

Highest praises
Highest praises to everything that covers our heads
Highest praises to the light that lives inside of you
Highest praises to the great spirit
The owner of the womb
The owner of the day
The owner of the night
The owner of breath

Highest praises to the dead
That sit at the foot of god
May they rest in peace
May they rest in peace
May they rest in peace
May they rest in peace

And to the oceans, the rivers, the gentle breeze,
The storming thunder, the earth, paths and crossroads
The herbs and medicines, snow-capped mountains
And to all the elements
We give them our respect, and our gratitude

To be amongst them
By whatever name they might be called, or worshiped
Our humility is our gift and our birthright
As it is for every human
Growing as a seed under light of sun and moon

And to our children we give our gratitude and our respect
For we are the ancestors of a coming age
A new age by whom we will be called
The ancient ones.

Carolyn Brandy
San Francisco Bay Area

A Prayer Born of Sacred Oral Traditions and Always, Inescapably, the Written Text

I thank Ishtar-Iya Nla-Shekhinah, She Who Dwells Within; Yemaya-Olokun-Tanit, guardians of the ocean; and for keeping me rooted, Asherah, essence of the trees, the seas and the sacred poles, worshiped in the Temple and the high places until She was thrown out of the temple (and worshiped underground.) Gratitude to She Who* still lives in our sacred texts; Obatala and Hochmah/Sophia, gods of wisdom; Esu, who guides our comings and goings; Quan Yin, goddess of love, mercy and compassion; She Who is *rechem rachamim* (womb of compassion), and ancestress warrior-prophet-poet-judge Deborah, *eshet lapidot*, fiery woman, keeper of the flame...

Oya and Lilith, winds of change, help us, too, to be catalysts of cultural transformation, at a time when the world needs clear vision, truthful speech and courageous acts. For teaching us the power of words, for infusing us all with aṣẹ and ruach, lifeforce and breath, and the energy and inspiration to do this work, we thank you. Aṣẹ.

D'vorah J. Grenn
Napa, California

*Thanks to Judy Grahn for her classic "She Who" poems—"Grahn's title evokes a goddess figure yet might also be the secret tribal name of everywoman" – Alicia Ostriker, Stealing The Language, © 1986.

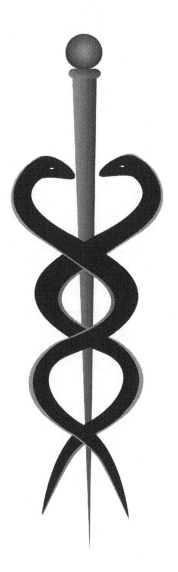

Introduction

This book reflects a decade of my listening to women's voices and bringing together women from different spiritual and cultural traditions to pray, play and celebrate their lives and their relationships with deity. The volume has also been driven by my own connection to Spirit, my questions about Her mysteries, my constant, impossible desire to define Her, and the wish to share the energies and essences of both public and private ceremonies and rituals of which I have been a part over the past fifteen years.

My passion for compiling these sacred words arose out of the desire I see in other women, and men, to unite with Her, and out of the need to proclaim more loudly and more often the sacred qualities of women's everyday lives and words.

Since the first Talking to Goddess manuscript, published in 2007 with the work of 28 contributors, this book has grown to include the work of 72 women, whose voices call out to Her from many parts of the world through stark and devotional poetry, prose, invocation, song and chant.

I am greatly indebted to these women, who believed in and supported this project, generously contributing their germinal* work and energy to bring it to life. The prayers contained herein are original works by the authors; a number of them were written expressly for this book. Some women thought it important to bring back work they had done years ago to bring awareness to a new generation; others were kind enough to share glimpses of forthcoming books and articles.

I especially thank Judy Grahn, Luisah Teish and Dianne Jenett, for inspiring and conspiring, and for their generosity in contributing their arts, both written and visual, to this project. My deepest gratitude to them, and to the Writers Egbe of Ile Orunmila Oshun, as well as to Kris Brandenburger and Cosi Fabian for unfailing support. Thanks, too, to Betty De Shong Meador for sharing her work on Nisaba in this volume, and always, for bringing Enheduanna's words—the first written record of a woman talking to her personal goddess—to us at this moment in time. One could not ask for a more stimulating, caring family of writers, friends, colleagues and spirit sisters and brothers. I thank the women closest to me for never letting me forget the unquestionable need to have, in the words of Virginia Woolf, a room of one's own.

The encouraging words and excited responses I have gotten from many women, both those in this book and those who will be contributing to Talking To Goddess, Volume 2 reflect our yearning for Her, for Spirit/uality, however one envisions these entities. The ongoing need and hunger for both human and divine connectedness and interrelationship is evidenced in the women's writings. Their work speaks to both the very personal desire for spiritual union, as well as the wider human need for such connection—a need which, gone unmet, erupts in ever-increasing alienation and violence.

I hope the deep conversations with Spirit in this book will impact readers as much as it has the writers... from those who occasionally remember to talk to Her to those who begin our day with prayer, from those who only meditate at times of crisis or deep grief, to those whose lives are built around worship and devotion. Reading each others' work has helped us—and certainly, this editor—to stop in the midst of our daily busyness, to remember to pay attention to what really matters.

This anthology contains prayers to the Mother-Father God, Olokun, Nisaba, Kali, Shekhinah, Saraswati and Great Mother, to the orishas, West African goddesses Oshun, Yemaya and Oya; to Durga and Mukambika, to the dakinis, the matrikas, the ancient prophets; to O-yuki-san of Japan, Inanna-Ishtar, Guan Yin, Qadesha, White Tara. Herein too reside a variety of pagan and wiccan blessings, prayers to and musings on Mary, Mary Magdalene and the Black Madonna, Dark Mother, Queen of the Night and La Malinche, and writings on Spiderwoman, First Mother, Earth Mother. There is poetry celebrating women and political poetry written to help put our world back into balance, and performed over the last several years in a wide range of venues. This work has been seen and heard from the theatre to the street, from colleges to festivals, and from seasonal rituals, bembes, pujas and other religious services to a wide array of public and private secular ceremonies.

It includes prayers for healing and peace, to the best and worst in us, for countries, peoples and Nature; blessings for babies, new projects and over meals, to honor ancestors and invoke the Divine in a range of situations and for many different reasons; to honor the memories of women erased, wounded, killed or otherwise silenced. Some of the writings sacralize sexuality and some bring humor to the conversation.

I believe readers will see in these pages how She, the Sacred Feminine, touches and infuses our lives in many profound, simple and complex ways, every day—whether in worldly or incorporeal form—and how she manifests in and through us.

This book also reflects my thealogy, my philosophy on our relationships with divine Spirit and divine humans. I developed it in the course of writing my dissertation, "For She Is A Tree of Life: Shared Roots Connecting Women to Deity." The values it embodies directed my editorial choices as I created this anthology, and so I include it here. This thealogy:

- believes we can only connect with deity by working towards a unity of human spirit, and through compassionate human interaction;

- holds women's and men's lives, minds and bodies as sacred;
- regards women's monthly cycles as evidence of a non-violent, sacred covenant with the Divine, a contract of co-creation with God and the universe;
- encourages the creation of a covenant with God by both women and men on a daily basis, grounded in the belief that one may enter into a direct conversation or relationship with the Divine at any time, without need for an intermediary;
- supports the analysis and critique of traditional sacred texts—and the creation of personal prayers and new liturgy—by all those interested in such explorations;
- believes in making knowledge more accessible and smashing the idea that access to God/dess can or should be controlled through a chosen few;
- encompasses a view of sexuality and gender preference as sacred;
- asks that we regulate ourselves to maintain a high ethical standard, without needing fear of divine retribution as a controlling mechanism;
- seeks ways of expressing our faith which are non-exclusionary, non-judgmental and which can cross traditional religious 'lines' to bring disparate groups together to worship as one, while allowing for cultural diversity;

- embodies an active recognition of deity as having both female and male aspects, whenever God is discussed as corporeal; and
- honors the power of the individual to make change – at every opportunity, in every moment.

One of my greatest hopes in publishing this anthology is that we—women as well as men—will again be able to recognize and revere the Sacred Feminine in ourselves and each other, that we will see it as a way to enrich and not polarize our lives.

I could not complete this Introduction without expressing my deep gratitude to Xochipala Maes Valdez for her invaluable help and guidance in navigating the challenging, at times mysterious waters of graphic design, layout and publishing. Without her wise editorial eye, insightful comments and project timelines, this book would not have embodied my values as completely as it now does, and would have taken far longer to complete.

And always, much love and appreciation to my family, who provide a supportive container for my life, and to Marc, my partner of the heart, who keeps the means of production, from computers to caffeine, running smoothly at all hours of day and night. His calm, loving presence and infinite patience hold me through multiple simultaneous deadlines, and all the demands and delights of an overflowing, intense, nomadic life.

----

*Thanks to Judy Grahn for insisting we use an alternative to the male-centered word "seminal." In addition to not wanting to prolong the use of androcentric language, I use germinal here because it so aptly reflects the role of women as originators. It also holds my vision for this book as a generative source containing seeds for future growth as women share it in their own communities.

Opening
Invocation

may we embrace

Great Mother, Great Spirit, Great Mother-Father God
may we embrace
those whose deity is a talkative stone
a sacred tree or a reindeer
may we embrace
those whose deity is a complex historic story
of martyrdom, suffering and redemption
may we embrace
those whose deity is immanent in a dance of joy
in drum-song, or a literate tattoo carved in flesh
of sacred human body
knowing yours is the greatest of all bodies

Great Spirit, Great Father-Mother God, Great Mother
may we embrace
those whose deity is the keeping of just law
and may we embrace
those whose deity is the breaking of unjust law
may we embrace
those whose deity is a sexual being, and
those whose deity is a breath of sound, and
those whose deity is crafting a talisman of jewels

or a beautiful cloth, a painting in sand
of our lives as paintings in the wind
knowing yours is the gift of thoughtful action

Great Father-Mother God, Great Spirit, Great Dancing Mother
may we embrace
those whose deity drips gore
in the eternal bone yard
of the nonreality of any body
and may we embrace just sitting with all being
those whose deity is present in a tender kiss
of the baby god
and the blessing of all relationships
knowing you are the blood red web holding our short lives
on this long earth

Great Mother, Great Spirit, Great Father-Mother God
may we embrace
our own hearts
may our hearts stretch large
as wombs
as consciousness
as the river of life

you of the nebulae and the black holes
you of the microbes and spinning cells
you of the shimmering cosmic delight
may our hearts stretch toward your heart
you of the largest heart

may we embrace

Judy Grahn
Palo Alto, California

CONTRIBUTORS
Order of Conversations

A Glimpse
of History

Praise to Nisaba of Eresh
Goddess of Writing, Goddess of Grain

written by
Betty De Shong Meador

...who has brought the modern world translations of Enheduanna's prayers and hymns in **Inanna, Lady of Largest Heart** *and in* **Princess, Priestess, Poet – the Sumerian Temple Hymns of Enheduanna.**

The rich written treasures of the Sumerian civilization have been deciphered and translated only in the past 50 to 75 years. Scholars have now been able to connect the origin of western civilization back to the land between the two rivers (the Tigris and the Euphrates,) to the original Sumerian culture whose ancestors first occupied that land around 5000 BCE.

In the third millennium territory of Umma, Nisaba became the personal goddess of the rulers. About the same time, Enheduanna's nephew, the powerful Akkadian king Naram-Sin, dedicated a mace head to Nisaba. King Shulgi in the Ur III dynasty at the end of the third millennium enlarged the literary canon with numerous hymns, even inserting one of his hymns into copies of Enheduanna's Temple Hymns, written three hundred years earlier. Whether Shulgi himself or his scribes wrote the hymns is unknown. In a poem praising himself, Shulgi says, "I am a knowledgeable scribe of Nisaba," and ends his poem, "Praise be to Nisaba."[i]

Nisaba had many attributes related to her primary features as goddess of grain and goddess of writing. In Temple Hymn 42, Enheduanna calls her "faithful woman exceeding in wisdom." Already mentioned was her close relationship to scholars and scholarly activities. Mathematics and astronomy were in her repertoire. She was said to be a "lady with cunning intelligence."[ii] She was the goddess of creative inspiration, goddess of creative mind.

She epitomized godly wisdom and the gift of learning. King Lipit-Eshtar wrote in a hymn to Nisaba these lines:

Nisaba, the woman radiant with joy
Faithful woman, scribe, lady who knows everything
Guided your fingers on the clay
Embellished the writing on the tablets
Made the hand resplendent with a golden stylus
The measuring rod, the gleaming surveyor's line,
The cubit ruler which gives wisdom
Nisaba lavishly bestowed on you [iii]

From Settlement to Script

The significance of the written sign in Sumer lay in its identification with the divine being, the sign being inseparable from the goddess herself. Naturally, the question arises, why was the goddess of grain also the divine being who gave writing as we know it to human beings? The answer may lie in the conjunction of grain cultivation with the building of early settled communities.

Archeological evidence indicates that in the period from 15,000 to 11,500 BCE, early occupants of the ancient Near East—Israel, Jordan, Lebanon, and Syria—experimented with the cultivation of grains that grew naturally in the wild around them. Agriculture that could sustain a community's food needs, however, required daily tending, technological skills, and a favorable conjunction of natural elements. Not until around 9000 BCE, were groups in the ancient Near East able to cultivate grain successfully enough to feed a whole village. With the added food supplies from hunting, herding, and fishing, they could then support year round settlements. The dependability of a stable community and an adequate food supply allowed additional time for the deliberate development of governance and religious practices, and for artistic expression.

By the late fourth millennium BCE, Nisaba had become the divine presence in life-sustaining grain. Its organized storage and equitable distribution required that transactions be recorded in some elementary fashion. Nisaba watched over the cultivation, storage, and distribution of grain and over the essential records. Her divine sanction formed the basis of organized community life.

Her essential role is described in a late third millennium hymn to the king Išbi-Erra of Isin that praises Nisaba "greater than all." Following are excerpts from this hymn:

The Lady – in the place which she approaches there is
    writing!.....
Nisaba, the place which you do not establish,
(There) humanity is not established, cities are not built,
The palace is not constructed, the king is not elevated,
The purification rites of the gods are not performed!

Nisaba, the place which you do not approach,
(There) no stall is constructed, no sheepfold erected,
The shepherd does not soothe the heart with the flute,
The tending staff is not set up, (the stall's) cleaning is not
    performed
The little shepherd does not churn the milk, does not
    shake the churn
From it, fat and cream do not issue,
And the table of the gods is (thus) not made perfect!.....

For Enlil, the king of all the lands,
You are his great storage room, you are his seal keeper.....

Your growth is indeed the furrow,
Your form is indeed the grown grain,
Your features, all of them, are good,
Your figure is indeed that grain! iv

----

i Jeremy Black, Graham Cunningham, Eleanor Robson, and Gábor Zólyomi, The Literature of Ancient Sumer (Oxford: Oxford University Press, 2004), 307.

ii Åke Sjöberg, "The Old Babylonian Edubba." Sumerological Studies in Honor of Thorkild Jacobsen (Chicago: University of Chicago Press, 1975), 175.

iii H.L.J. Vanstiphout, "Lipit-Eshtar's Praise in the Edubba." Journal of Cuneiform Studies 30 (1978), 33-61, l. 18ff.

iv Daniel Reisman, "A "Royal" Hymn of Išbi-Erra to the Goddess Nisaba." In Barry L. Eichler, ed., Kramer Anniversary volume (Kevelaer, Germany: Verlag Butzon and Bercker, 1976), 359.

Calling

Her In

Tatawari Taruama prayer

Deep breath. Feel the place our breaths meet in the middle of the circle feel the warmth of the fire on your face feel the warmth of the sun on your face breathe...

Tatawari Taruama Grandfather Grandmother of all things, please hear our prayers. We come to you in humble way. We give thanks for another day on this beautiful earth! We give thanks for all those who came before us, our ancestors, who believed in life enough to pass it on in love and generosity. For those who walked this earth whose names we don't remember. We pray and ask forgiveness for all the things we may have done to offend others past, present or future, we ask forgiveness of the standing tall ones the tree people, the winged ones the four-leggeds and all the creatures of the water for the ways we disregard their lives. Please help us to regain the balance we once knew.

Please help us to learn to share this earth again with all creation. We give thanks to the tree people who gave their life so we might have this fire. We thank the mother for this air we breathe for the sacred water that sustains this life. For all these things we give thanks!

We pray for the young ones all over the world that they may know they are loved and their life is unique and precious. Please guide the way of those unborn who journey to this earthly plane. Please bless those who for whatever reason are unable to pray for themselves. Help us to remember the sacredness of each moment. Allow us to feel the gift of life and to be kind to all our relations.

A-ho. May you walk in beauty until our paths cross again.

Charlie Toledo
Napa, California

Calling Olokun's Wife
Transmitted by Ohen Imene Nosokpikan,
for whom Olokun is male

"When you address Olokun at any time, you must first address Osanobua (the Supreme Being), then Olokun's wife, who is Ora in Edo; you call her to get him:"

Oraa O

Oraa O O

Oraa O

O O

Oraa O O O O

Ohen Imene Nosokpikan
(Nedra Williams)
Oakland, California

Blessing While Cooking

All that I have comes from my Mother!
I give myself over to this pot.
My thoughts are on the good,
the healing properties of this food.
My hands are balanced, I season well!

I give myself over to this pot,
Life is being given to me.
I commit to sharing, I feed others.
I feed She Who Feeds Me.

I give myself over to this gift.
I adorn this table with food.
I invite lovers and friends to come share.
I thank you for this gift.
All that I have comes from my Mother!

Chief Luisah Teish
Oakland, California

Call To Worship
(said before praying to Olokun)

O hand bell
O rattle
My beloved drum
We are about to visit the deep and to return
(Said three times)

I bring a hand bell
I bring a rattle
We have come to meet you, Oh, Owner of the Sea
(Repeat)

Ohen Imene Nosokpikan
(Nedra Williams)
Oakland, California

Olokun Prayer (unfinished)
For my Olokun, who is female

As I speak to you, Olokun, I greet Yemaya
Olodo Yemaya!
O mio Yemaya!
Tanit
Asherah
Mami Wata
NyamiNyami

I speak to ocean, bay and river,
all the water goddesses, spirits and deities
But mostly, I speak to you, Olokun

Said on crossing bodies of water

Malókun bu owo wa, Oba omí ju Oba òkè.
Jími tètè núwà o. Oba omí ju Oba òkè. Aṣẹ.

Olokun, we ask that you bring us abundance and prosperity,
Both spiritual and material.
We are asking you for what we need
to greet the world with clear minds and open hearts,
to live full, vibrant lives with all other beings...

Sharing, serving, interacting, reaching our highest
and deepest
selves
As we carry our destinies forward, on ancestors' shoulders
Unafraid to sit in our own power
to stand
and lie
and LIVE in it.

Oba omí ju Oba òkè.
The spirit of the Ocean is greater than the chief
the priestess*
of any land.

Let us never take for granted your power, Olokun
You, who intoxicates our senses
With your overwhelming beauty and strength

We are grateful for all the waters you are,
Great Ocean Mother
Your rhythmic tides and fickle currents
Your reliable, unpredictable waves

---

*Author's adaptation

Your promise of sustenance and threat of destruction
That keep us in love-hate relationship with You

Some humans argue that you are only in charge of the bottom
of the ocean and that Yemaya-Yemonja-Yemoja rules the top.

How absurd! How you must laugh.
Knowing you are the all,
and that Yemaya, too, is the all.

Great Ocean Spirit, Sacred Waters, Essence of Life...

Hold us, when we forget You...
Or ourselves.

D'vorah J. Grenn
Napa, California

Incantation to Goddesses of Life and the Waters

This invocation is based on my practice of meditation / incantation / movement.

A large circle of people chanted it while stepping sunwise in the Grandmother's Dance at the Pagan Alliance Festival in Berkeley, May 9, 2009. It seemed the right time to praise life, and to raise joy, strength, healing and blessings for transformation in these intense times. And, in the midst of a drought, to bless and make reverence to the Waters, the source of all Life.

Awei! We pour libation to this land and its ancestors here, and for the Huichiun Ohlone people on whose land we stand: May they live. Awei! Awei! Awei!

Awei! We pour libations to the ancestors of everyone here, and to the ancestors of all peoples, our relatives. May we live. Awei! Awei! Awei!

Awei! We pour libation for the welfare of all living beings, to the Whole, the Full Circle. May all live in peace and health and plenty. Awei! Awei! Awei!

We turn to salute and call on the Directions:

Awei! Grandmothers of the East, Dawn Beings, help us to rise in
optimism
Awei! Grandmothers of the South, Blaze of Day, strengthen our
hearts
Awei! Grandmothers of the West, Great Waters, lave and clarify
our souls
Awei! Grandmothers of the North, Deep Stone Roots, grant us
staying power
Awei! Divine Center, Original Source within all beings, illumine
and guide us
We bend to touch Mother Earth, our foundation: Awei! Awei!
Awei!
and salute the expanse of Sky with our raised hands: Awei!
Awei! Awei!

Now we chant and dance sunwise in the Grandmothers' Dance:

Om Paraashaktyai Swahaa	To divine power, offering reverence
Om Mahaadevyai	*O Great Goddess*
O Zhiva Swahaa	O Living Goddess, reverence
May we heal	*May we heal*

Omíyo Yemaya	Praises to Yemaya, Ocean Mother
Modupwé Iya	*Thanks O Mother*
Bless all living beings, Swahaa	Bless all living beings, our offering
Pachamama O	*O Earth Mother (Peru)*
Om Satyaa Svahaa	To Truth / Being, reverence
Sánanos, sanamos	*Heal us, we are healing*
Tamo pahaayai, Svahaa	Remove negativity, offering it up
Abhayamkari, abhayamkari	*Make fearless, make fearless*
Divyaayai Shobhanaa	Effulgent Radiance
Svaprakashaa	*Self-illumined Spirit*
Sri Vidya Svahaa	Blessed Wisdom, reverence
Ilumínanos, iluminamos	*Illuminate us, let us illuminate*
Open a way, swahaa	Open a way, offering reverence

Libéranos, Liberamos	*Free us, we are freeing*
Om Paraashaktyai Swahaa	To divine power, offering reverence
Om Mahaadevyai	*O great Goddess*

Max Dashú
Oakland, California

Note:

In the libations, Awei is a phonetic rendering of the original pronunciation of Ave, the honorific Latin salutation (as in Ave María). Each line in the chant is sung four times, then its chorus (in italics) also four times. Most of the chant draws on Goddess litanies in Sanskrit. It also calls on Zhiva, the Slavic Goddess of Life, the Orisha Yemaya in Yoruba, and the Quechua Earth Mother Pachamama, with a few lines in Spanish. You can hear a video of the chant at www.sourcememory.net/chants/litany.html.

The Grandmothers' Dance is an American Indian name for the worldwide circle dance of step-to-the-left, right-foot-steps-where-left-foot-stood.

Matrikas Invocation

Brahmani, you of the Great Revelation, we bow to you. Dressed in yellow of the newest day, you who make your enemies inert with the blessed water from your womblike pot, tonight make us inert in wonderment, open to receive your boons and blessings. Let us count with you upon your akshamala (rosary) the names of love and com-passion that you have manifested upon this earth. In our minds and hearts, we hold with you all the beings and spirits who have touched us through your golden visage, golden grace. We call upon you to be with us, bringing your red lotus seat to fire our imaginations, and your swan companion to grant us the wisdom of ages. Om, Brahmani, namostute namah.

Maheshvari, woman of the bull, carrier of the trident, and seer of the moon, we honor you as manifest courage, strength and guided, transformational rage. You who are colored white, remind us of our pure potential. You who are four-handed, bring us the knowings of the four directions, the bounty of the earth, air, fire and water. You who have five faces, each with three eyes, see with us into the past, present and future; hold us in your gaze as we venture in our individual and collective quest for wholeness, righteousness, and sublime adoration of truth and beauty. You who in name manifests the supreme power located in the heart that unites all opposites, we bow to you. Om Maheshvari namostute namah.

Kaumari, goddess of the springtime, of the melting snow and birthing doe; you who are six-faced, come to us with your news of foreign lands, discoveries, reverie, and insight. Hold us in your sight as we enter into the dreamtime of ritual, seeking to commune with all those who have birthed innocence and peace. You whose memory is first in the minds of ancients, come to us bringing the many-colored eyes of your peacock to help us understand. Lend us your spear so that we may pierce the veil of ignorance. From your four hands, give us the gifts of perseverance, humility, passion and desire; and accept our offerings this evening of honesty, devotion, reverence, and respect. To you who resides under the fig tree, She who is ever strong, we bow. Om Kaumari namostute namah.

Vaishnavi, we call to you. She who rides a Garuda to the crest of the waves and the valleys of grief, She whose beautiful visage marks enlightenment, be with us now. Honor us with the long-sighted goal of your cakra thrown in the name of unity and common purpose. Bring us the power of your club, bow, and sword to deter our egos and false illusions. Sound for us your conch shell so that we may hear the resonance of perspectives garnered from about the globe in support of sustainability, nurturance, mindfulness and peace. To you who comes to us in the colors of dawning preservation, we bow. Om Vaishnavi namostute namah.

Varahi, goddess with the head of a boar, we beseech you to let us ride with you upon your elephant tonight. Let us ride with you in your search for reason, in your quest for the ultimate sacrifice, in your march towards responsibility and justice. You who are adorned with ornaments made of coral, bring to us your knowledge of the sea, that primordial ocean of bliss from which you come, that reservoir of infinite love, that place of belly-wrenching righteousness and surreal splendor. You who represent the color of clouds before illumination, you who kill the enemies of freedom, you who devour darkness, be with us now. Om Varahi namostute namah.

Chamunda, goddess of all reckoning, you who inspire fear with a glance, you who licks the wounds of asuras (demons) as you laugh and trample them to death, come to us drunk on the blood of life, inebriated on the wings of hope. Your skeleton red reminds us of our origins in Mama's darkness as your digambari pleasure makes us tell the need for nothingness. Garbed in space, your hair aflame in a cobra tiara, you dance on cremation grounds and bring joy to despair, laughter to sorrow, mirth to uneasy embarrassment. Holding your kapala (skull cup) full of your enemies' blood, you choose life at every juncture and will us to do the same. Divine mother of might who rides the owl of death, the corpse of ultimate transformation, be with us now. Om Chamunda namostute namah.

Aindri, She whose four arms and thousand eyes radiate from a golden visage, open us to the expanse of richness that lies within. Holding your thunderbolt, you are a flash of cosmic power; please lend us your insight. With spear and club in your hands you conquer ill-will and pierce the walls of deceit. Let us, oh goddess, do the same. Om Aindri namostute namah.

Mahalakshmi, wisdom keeper and guardian of secrets, be among us. From your reserves of kindness, fill us a basket of daring, of yearning, of helpfulness, and of home-spaces filled with sweetness. Come to us radiant to remind us each of our own gifts and gratitudes, of our own capacity and caring. You who are gifted in making dreams reality, we ask for your benediction, your blessings and your boons in our troubled times. Om Mahalakshmi namostute namah.

Chandra Alexandre
San Francisco, California

Invocation to Inanna-Lilith-Shekhinah...

She of all knowing, dark wisdom... She of the deep abyss,
   snake's descent, owl's knowing... woman of the dark,
   the light.
We praise you, we stand in awe marveling at the myriad sur-
   prises you hold in store for us, always respectful of your
   power, your mystery.

Lilith-Inanna-Shekhinah, we worship you, in all your aspects;
   we sing your name.

Walk with us as we yearn to serve you... Never let us forget
   your presence in, around and through us, as we seek to
   proclaim and praise you in every corner of the world, in
   your many guises, by every name.
Walk with us as we love you, when we are angered by you,
   when we fail to comprehend you and when we renew our
   resolve to serve...

Be patient with us as we must be with ourselves, each other...
   holding your presence even when in doubt or despair.
Let us walk into this new millenium as a time of healing, of
   casting new roles for ourselves and others, weaving new
   threads of oneness and wonder.

Inanna-Lilith-Shekhinah, keeper of the mystery
Be with us through ecstasy and harmony
  through death and destruction
You who were given the setting up of lamentations,
the care of children,
the rejoicing of the heart,
the giving of judgments,
the stirring of sexuality,
the making of decisions.

In the eye of this wisdom, rising forth from the power of your
  being, your foresight, your intent... how is it we ever got
  lost, taken over, subsumed?
How did we e'er become convinced we were not worthy to
  serve you, that you were the god/not the goddess? How
  did you/we allow ourselves to be sidetracked, trampled,
  silenced and burned?
Allow us always to remember our inner strengths, to come
  from a place of understanding.
  Let us not be swayed from our goals.
  Work with us, inspire us, protect us as we weave your
  work—our work.

Help us, Sweet Dark Lady of the Night, holy winged figure of
  the light—rageful, wise judge, warmest heart, soulful

visionary... Highest Priestess of the T/temples to whom every knee must bend and every tongue give homage.

For it is your word we write now upon the doorpost of our
  house and upon our gates,
Your word, acts, images and thoughts we share, grow mad at,
  weep with and seek to learn...and learn from.

It is you who makes rise our greatest laughter, happiness,
  peace and compassion, who sees and gives us our greatest
  rage and storm, temper and venom;
You from whom and with whom we learn to combine these
  things in the best ways possible...

Sweet, dark goddess/es of the earth and sky, river and moun-
  tain, night and day, Heaven & Hell.
We seek to embody your passion, your wisdom, your strength.
Be with us now.

D'vorah J. Grenn
Written in Jerusalem, 1999

Invoking the Prophet Women of Ancient Israel

We long for the insights of the female visionaries of ancient Israel, whose prophetic contributions were recognized by the sages of the Talmud.

These include Sarah, Miriam, Devorah, Hannah, Avigail, Huldah & Esther.

MIRIAM   Charismatic spiritual and political leader you challenged male authority from childhood; and taught through ecstatic music and dance.
You nourished us in the desert—watering our bodies and souls.

Guide us now, through another wilderness of confusion, showing us the way to restore feminine energy to a wounded planet.

DEBORAH Great warrior, judge and Mother in Israel, your fiery example inspires us to take action.
We long to know more of your words and yearn to take your poetry into our hearts and minds.

We need your energy to sacralize the political and create leaders that embody your prophetic leadership.

HANNAH Woman of personal prayer, your petition is our model
for individual appeals to the divine.
You called out directly to God for help, transcending
the conventional service.

*We join your davenning now, so that we might be empowered to
attract divine healing into the barren places in our lives.*

AVIGAIL Forceful woman of Carmel, you foresaw David's
future; feeding and welcoming the outlaw chief
when his life was in jeopardy.
Becoming his wife in hard times, before he was
King and Psalmist, you supported the emergence
of genius.

*Send us your insight so we might have the strength to trust and
follow our intuitions.*

HULDAH Huldah, preacher at the Southern gates of the Temple;
you were consulted on important religious matters,
like your cousin Jeremiah.
You, whose teaching comes to us in your advice to
King Josiah are needed now for the creation of new
ways of learning.

Help us find the deep learning of enlightenment and peace

ESTHER   Gentle Queen, with the premonitory knowledge that
                 propelled you to save your people.
                 Whether you are historical or mythological, we are
                 touched by your story.
                 How you must have feared your awesome destiny,
                 overcoming the fear with transcendent faith.

**Bless us with inner strength to overcome the obstacles that block
us from fulfilling our sacred assignments.**

> *Rabbi Leah Novick*
> *Monterey, California*

Mandala of the Five Dakinis
(adapted from the Tibetan by Vicki Noble)

Preparation:
I light five candles in the cardinal directions and center—blue in the east, yellow in the south, red in the west, green in the north, and white in the center. I sit facing east. Using a mala (a Tibetan rosary of 108 beads), I count mantras to clear my mind and open my heart. I chant OM AH HUM over and over again; it hollows me out. I make intentions to generate the sweet loving kindness of a breast-feeding mother so that the prayers I make may flow out of me and be of benefit to all beings.

(Ring bell)
Great Goddess of the East, Blue Vajra Dakini, I ask your presence in my life at this time. I invite you to remember me, as I vow to remember you with praise and sacred offerings. Water Goddess of the rivers, lakes, oceans, springs, and streams, please answer my prayer. Wisdom Dakini bring your mirror and show me perfect clarity. Banish anger from my heart and put compassion in its place. Grant me the gift of mirror-like wisdom. Remove poison from the blood and lymph, and pour the contents of your precious vase into the top of my head and down into my heart for healing. Build an indestructible pillar at the center of my being, and seal it with your adamantine

Diamond of truth. Re-establishing your element within me, make me whole.

(I snap fingers to acknowledge the fusion between me and the Blue Vajra Dakini)

(Ring bell)
Great Goddess of the South, Yellow Ratna Dakini, I ask your presence in my life at this time. I invite you to remember me, as I vow to remember you with praise and sacred offerings. Earth Mother of the mountains, hills, forests, valleys, and fields, please answer my prayer. Banish arrogance and insecurity from my breast and put generosity in its place. Grant me the wisdom of equanimity. Remove tumors and growths from my flesh, and pour the contents of your precious vase into the top of my head and down into my heart for healing. Build an indestructible pillar at the center of my being, and seal it with your golden Jewel of abundance. Re-establishing your element within me, make me whole.

(I snap my fingers to acknowledge the fusion)

(Ring bell)
Great Goddess of the West, Red Padma Dakini, I ask your presence in my life at this time. I invite you to remember me, as I

vow to remember you with praise and sacred offerings. Fire Goddess of the burning embers, lightning, volcano, creativity and sexuality, please answer my prayer. Banish craving and obsession from my heart and put warm presence in its place. Grant me the wisdom of discrimination. Remove blockages to the circulation of heat through my channels, and pour the contents of your precious vase into the top of my head and down into my heart for healing. Build an indestructible pillar at the center of my being, and seal it with your lush red Lotus of immortality. Re-establishing your element within me, make me whole.

(I snap my fingers to acknowledge the fusion)

(Ring bell)

Great Goddess of the North, Green Karma Dakini, I ask your presence in my life at this time. I invite you to remember me, as I vow to remember you with praise and sacred offerings. Sky-Going Goddess of the cyclones, gentle breezes, hurricanes, breath, and prana, please answer my prayer. Banish jealousy and anxiety from my nervous system and put spontaneous accomplishment in its place. Grant me the wisdom of letting things unfold naturally. Remove obstacles to deep breathing, and pour the contents of your precious vase into the top of my head and down into my heart for healing. Build an indestructible pillar at the center of my being, and seal it with your Amazon's Double Axe. Re-establishing your element within me, make me whole.

(I snap my fingers to acknowledge the fusion)

(Ring bell)
Great Goddess of the Center, White Buddha Dakini, I ask your presence in my life at this time. I invite you to remember me, as I vow to remember you with praise and sacred offerings. Pregnant Mother of the great Yoni, emptiness, open space, meditative bliss, and every possibility, please answer my prayer. Banish avoidance and forgetfulness from my consciousness and put acceptance in its place. Grant me the wisdom of spacious accommodating presence. Remove mental obstacles or deterioration, and pour the contents of your precious vase into the top of my head and down into my heart for healing. Build an indestructible pillar at the center of my being, and seal it with your great Wheel of Natural Law. Re-establishing your element within me, make me whole.

(I snap my fingers to acknowledge the fusion)

Gratitude:
I ring my Tibetan bell and chant the mantra BAM HA RI NI SA [BAM: center, HA: East, RI: South, NI: West, and SA: North], pic-

turing the mandala of Dakinis around me and inside of me. Feeling the wonder, I rest in enjoyment for as long as I can.

Dedication of Merit:
I ask that all merit (healing, empowerment, protection, health, happiness, prosperity, etc.) be shared with all beings. "May all beings realize the Dakini. May all beings know true happiness and an end to suffering. May there be peace on earth. Blessed Be."

[I ring bells, dismiss the directions, and blow out the candles, in gratitude.]

Vicki Noble
Santa Cruz, California

An Invocation

I pay homage to the Goddess
I call in the Priestess, the Oracle, the Aunt, the Sister,
   the Warrior
I call in the Scholar, the Healer, the Comic, the Artist, the Lover
I call to you, Goddess, in your many forms
To join hands with the Great Mother, to whom we so often call
Come join hands in the circle
Bring all of You into the divine conversation
Reflect upon us the many honorable and needed
  expressions of Woman
So that we may walk in Your ways

Christine Brooks
Santa Cruz, California

Holy Mother, Shechinah Soul

Holy Mother Shechinah Soul,
Rachamema
Compassion fills Your Womb of Love
T'hallelu hah!

Holy Mother Shechinah Soul
Mikor Hayim
Fountain of Life Flows from You
Uv'shavten mayim.

Holy Mother Shechinah Soul
Shechinat- El
On wings of light we soar to You,
Natchil L'hitpalel.

Holy Mother Shechinah Soul
Eheyeh Asher Eheyeh
You were, You are, You'll always be,
Gam anachnu Nihiyeh.

Holy Mother Shechinah Soul
Melechet Shamayim

You rule skies and earth with a gentle hand,
Borchi et Yerushalayim.

Holy Mother Shechinah Soul
Rachmana Ya
You heal the wounds of a heavy heart,
Ayl Na Raphana La.

Holy Mother Shechinah Soul
Be'er L'chai Roi
I drink deep of Your love
Ki At Emadi.

Prayer to the First Mother

Mother, first Mother
fill our hearts with the love
that goes back to the first love
which made your heart burst open
with the creative life force
from which we were born

Mother, first Mother
fill us with that pure love
give us the capacity to understand
so that our hearts hold compassion
and we can see with eyes
unjudging of our brothers and sisters
and the knowledge that we all come
from you
born of that first love

Mother, first Mother
fill us with your love
so that we may in turn give it
to one another
and in the giving
see it grow bigger and bigger

until we are all one
human family
in your love

Mother, first Mother
fill us with that pure love
so that we hear the whispers of your voice
in the wind and
in the rustle of the corn as it grows
telling us what we need to know
to live in harmony
on this Earth

Mother, first Mother
fill our hearts with love
and our eyes with your truth
so that when we die
we become part of you
and your love
flesh and bones returning to you
returning to the cycle of
the creative force
from which we came

Pennie Opal Plant, 1992
Albany, California

Litany of the Black Madonna

She is the Our Lady of the Tree, Rock, Sea and Cave
Beloved Mother of Wisdom, You are Black and Beautiful!

She is the Madonna of Fire and Water
Beloved Mother of Wisdom, You are Black and Beautiful!

She is the Madonna of High Places, and of places deep within the earth.
Beloved Mother of Wisdom, You are Black and Beautiful

She reminds us of cycles of the seasons, honoring the above and below and the passages in between
Beloved Mother of Wisdom, You are Black and Beautiful

She is the Throne, the Seat of our Wisdom
Beloved Mother of Wisdom, You are Black and Beautiful

She reminds us of the Earth as Source, of Female as source, Goddess as source. She blesses us with her holy blood and sanctifies our own blood.
Beloved Mother of Wisdom, You are Black and Beautiful

She helps us find the Black Madonna within us all.
Beloved Mother of Wisdom, You are Black and Beautiful

She is fierce to protect us, compassionate to hold us and hear our prayers.
Beloved Mother of Wisdom, You are Black and Beautiful

She is Queen and Virgin, one unto herself. She is inviolate. She is rising up.
Beloved Mother of Wisdom, You are Black and Beautiful

She unites opposites. She brings balance.
Beloved Mother of Wisdom, You are Black and Beautiful

She is the face of our First Mother, our Oldest Mother, our African Mother. She reminds us that we are all Sisters, Brothers.
Beloved Mother of Wisdom, You are Black and Beautiful

She is Mother, Mother of All, Mother of All that is.
Beloved Mother of Wisdom, You are Black and Beautiful!

Mary Beth Moser
Vashon Island, Washington

Stardust

I was made to dream
of the ancient maternal ancestor
without name
who travelled
effortlessly on the common
wind

My mother's mother's
mother
and back still
to reach the lacquered night
of West Africa

I was made to dream
of her mother's
lineage

until I teetered on the cusp
of human becoming

until
the stardust mother
titillated my dreams

and her matter
became
my
third
eye

and

being made to dream
dreaming
as I was being made

I awoke
professing
blessings, blessings, blessings

for the
one mother
beyond
articulation
and
conception

blessings, blessings
blessings

for the primordial
contraction
without beginning
and
without end

Sauda Burch
Oakland, California

The Great Mother

The Great Mother does not care about us.
Our personal lives do not move her.
Her concerns are
The raising up of mountains,
The wheeling of stars in the heavens,
The nightly rising of the moon,
The turning of the seasons.
We are so small, so ephemeral, our plight is less than a bother,
Not even a pesky mosquito to swat aside.
She is not kind,
but neither is she cruel.
She is busy.

Hymn to Nyx

She opens her wings of night,
Welcoming all who receive her favor.
Stars sparkle in the fathomless dark behind her,
And we climb into her embrace.

Mother of the dusk daughters,
Keepers of the golden apples,
You know what is treasure

and what is mere riches,
What is beauty
and what is only show.

We cannot know you
But we keenly feel the loss
When you draw away from us.
Without the refuge of
your enfolding wings
We wander, frustrated and lost,
Missing the misty path of night pearls
You illuminate for us.

You show the way.
No.
You are the way.
All praises to Nyx,
the guide, the protector, the healer.

Maya Spector
Menlo Park, California

The Moon is Her Beauty Mark –
A call to remember our Mother

Have you seen our Mother? When she sees all her little children running to her she opens her gigantic arms and gathers us up like chicks. Back in her arms again, worlds appear, disappear, and reappear upon the rise and fall of her breasts. Her honey milk flows and flows and we are nourished. It tastes so sweet.

Trees spontaneously spring from her, for she is a tree of life to all those who embrace her. And those who embrace her are blessed indeed. Guardian oaks grow from her shoulders pillars of strength for her children. Her breasts are orchards full of fruit for every single one of her little ones. Golden apples tumble from her armpits. Delicious fruits fall into our little pink mouths. The rust-red madrone of her calves is as smooth as silk for sliding down from volcano peaks through green and gold hillsides. She laughs brilliant, red, succulent pomegranates and you can see her bright teeth are flowering dogwood. Her womb, our warm red bed.

Can you hear our Mother singing? Birds are born upon her song. Redwing black birds, and opal-white doves, and red breasted robins, and purple-sapphire ravens fly right out of her songs! My favorite song is the redwing black bird symphony—all black with flashes of red winging a community of sound. I think seagulls are Mama's favorite. Children in the midst of cities love their sound it lets them smell the sea even while playing on a blacktop playground. Mama likes the vultures too taught them their own sacred song of silence because they are ones willing to be death's gardeners and fertilize garden earth. Mama much honors those who are willing to clean up after death. There is no where Mama is not.

Do you smell the scent of our Mother? That intoxicating scent of cinnamon and gardenia flying from her skirts as she moves upon her sandy shores, leaving footprints of frankincense and myrrh. Aloes spring up in the wake of her footsteps. When it is dark we can still find our way by smelling her trail. Smell the cedar? Smell the pine? Smell the redwood musk? Smell the sea? We are getting closer every second. There! See how her cypress hair blows to one side? And pink rose petals flutter from her ears lobes like shimmering pearl earrings.

Do you feel our Mother? She feels so comforting. Let us practice the wonder of living life in tune with the seasons and moons of our Mother's body. Let us knit dresses of her cherry blossoms and dance again the dance of the unbroken circle. Let us rejoice, and sing again in circle the songs of liberation and freedom! You remember don't you? How we sang the soil, the seed, the rain, the sun, the harvest? Remember how dragonflies circled our mother's head in a multi-winged halo? The butterflies made crowns for our heads also, happy to rest there even while we played hide and seek between the worlds. Then we swam in rivers thick with salmon swimming against our thighs. Feeling so good is being a part of our Mother's world. There is never a time when she is not with us, only seasons when we ourselves are either aware of her or not. But she is always there.

Let us celebrate our Mother's body! And her skin that is every color she ever made. Amazing! Isn't she? The rainbows and stardust of her skin make me want to cry. Like when her skin shines sky-blue, then new-leaf-green, then sun-yellow, all in the same day? My favorite days are the deep umber brown when her skin glows from the inside out. Most of the time she is as black as black can be. I heard we all used to be as black as she. Her ebony skin is the galaxy, the milky way scattered across the velvet blackness of her back; along her spine, infinite constellations, infinite pathways of wisdom; the moon is her beauty-mark.

Remember that time when we thought we were lost, but she gathered up our tribes in her ochre-red body and carried us safely across the abyss? Then came her days of glowing cobalt blue and poppy orange those days of healing old wounds with her balm of new life. Her flaming heart transformed our fears.

Then we praised her and touched her cheeks and hands, and rubbed the souls of all her feet with olive oil.

She has other kinds of days too—when we cannot recognize the colors at all—times when she is righting things that are wronged. We know our Mother is made up of love, and we also know she is fierce beyond all imagining. The sea is her medicine bag. Her fault lines her drawing board. Her skies are her tool box. She is the designer of everything. She is the wind in our hair when we ride the wild horses of our dreams. She is Our Lady of Everything.

We find her image in honor of her everywhere. Those of us who know her, cannot help but make words and art as greetings cards for her. From her cosmic dressing room she emerges, in the colors and shapes and signs of her peoples and lands. Sometimes she has many arms and legs, sometimes she slays the demons, sometimes she beats the drum, sometimes she descends, sometimes she flies, always, she births. Always she loves. Always she forgives. She is the mother of all and of everywhere. She is the Mother of God. She is the Mother of us. Through her, all comes into being and in time we are taken back into her body. We may dream of what she does with us from there, but who really knows? We could say she is one, we could say she is many, we could call her by a hundred million names, or we could just cry out MAMA! She answers to all of her names.

Reverend Shiloh Sophia McCloud
Healdsburg, California

Our Mother

Our Mother, who art within us,
   We celebrate your many names.
   Your wisdom come. Your will be done,
   Unfolding from the depths of us.
Each day You give us all that we need.
   You remind us of our limits and we let go.
   You support us in our power and we act with courage.
For you are the dwelling place within us,
   the empowerment around us, and the celebration among us.
As it was in the very beginning, may it be now.

The Divine Trinity

In the name of the Mother of All Living,
   (Touch your womb center in honor of the mother's intimate
   connection to the origins of life.)

and of the Divine Daughter,
   (Touch your breasts in honor of the daughter's developing
   body.)

and of the Wise Old Woman,
(Touch your eyes in honor of the wise inner vision acquired
through the accumulation of years.)

As it was in the very beginning, may it be now.
(Open your arms to receive All That Is.)

Patricia Lynn Reilly
Western Michigan

A Midwife's Meditation for Healing the Motherwound

Take a deep breath in and let it go to the center of your body.
Feel the ebb and flow of your breath and the expansion of
   your belly.
Let the belly be full and soft; let the heart be open to healing;
And let the mind feel its connection to the preciousness of life
   all around you.

Imagine that are surrounded by a fine golden light.
In this light are your guides, your guardian angels, and the
   spirits of your ancestors
They are sending you love and healing
They are sending you grace and blessings
They are sending you hope and renewal.

Breathe in their love and healing; breathe out your fear and
   doubt.
Breathe in their faith and courage; breathe out what does not
   serve you.

You are a child of spirit.
You are a child of earth
You are a child of your mother.

Your earthly mother who loved you
Your Divine Mother who blessed you
Your earthly mother who abused you
Your Divine Mother who saved you.
Your earthly mother who abandoned you
Your Divine Mother who sheltered you
Your earthly mother who raised you
Your Divine Mother who taught you
Your earthly mother who healed you.

Breathe in and follow the energy signature
Pulsing at the center of your belly
Follow the energy cord resting at the place of your navel
And feel the umbilical connection to the being who is your
    birth mother.

Breathe in and feel the sound of her heartbeat
Breathe in and feel the softness of her womb
Breathe in and feel the rocking of her movement.

Whoever you are and however you came here
You entered through the body of a woman.
Whoever you are and however you got here
Your first home was a space beneath her heart.

She is your gateway to life upon this planet.
She is the matrix for bodily existence.
She is the first being who should have offered you love.
Whether you were carried in war or peace, love or hope, grief
or depression
Your first home was the body of your mother.

Whether you are the child of rape and rejection, joyous love or
bitter longing
You are blood of her blood, bone of her bone, and flesh of
her flesh.

May your heart soften in gratitude towards the one who fed
you with her life.
May you pause and reflect on the suffering of her body.
May you acknowledge the gift of the legacy of her flesh.

Perhaps she betrayed this sacred charge
And all you know of her is that she carried you in her body
Perhaps she was the first to abuse and torture you
And all you know of her legacy is hatred, jealousy, shame and
belittlement.

If so,
Know that in the moment that you first entered form
The light of the Great Mother rested briefly in your body

Her radiance filled and surrounded you as she sung you
   out of the ether
Blessing you with power and protection, healing and love.

Your Divine Mother will never leave or abandon you.
She who nurtures and shelters, inspires and teaches, guides
   and protects,
Rested briefly in the body of your mother
Rested in you
And in the bodies of all the women who have ever loved you.
She is always here and She is always with you.

Remember always that you are her child
Remember always that She is your mother.

Breathe in her love and protection
Breathe in what heals and holds you
Breathe out what does not serve

Honor and praise to the mysteries of the womb
Honor and praise to the bearers of children
Honor and praise to the sacredness of life.
Honor and praise to our Divine Mother.

Arisika Razak
San Francisco Bay Area

To Mother, My Goddess

Mother, my Goddess,
I feel your presence in my heart

When I close my eyes,
I see your presence before me, surrounding me, enveloping
    me.
You softly whisper words of hope and encouragement,
And I cannot stop my tears of gratitude.

When my inner eyes are open,
All I see is the perfection and beauty of an intricately woven
    life.
You have been guiding me and protecting me all along,
And I am awed by the majestic silent power of your love

Even in my darkest moments, in the midst of struggle and
    suffering,
I can still continue to walk my path.
I can still be who I am, feeling joy and peace.
It is because of your presence, Mother, my Goddess.

Please help us continue to open our hearts even when faced
    with betrayal.

Please give us the strength to live through and learn from our
    challenges.

May all one of us find your love in our hearts.
May all of us share the abundance that you bring forth.
May your divine love, peace and joy prevail on Earth.

Amana Oh
California

Prayer to Mother Earth

Mother Earth, today we call you:
Great living planet,
Gaia,
Goddess,
Guide us
to sanctify the air, which is your breath,
to purify the water, which is your life's flow,
to edify the fire, which is your energy
to fructify the earth, which is your body.

Judith Laura
Washington, D.C. environs

The Divine Mother

A thousand tiny petals in my heart
Colorful, joyful, complete
Her hands enter my heart
Elevating the floral essence through me
Sprinkling gently
Fragrant roses cascade over my head
Filling my hands with abundance
There is no desire or longing
Only peace, stillness
To be with my Mother again!

Michele Arista, Spring 1998
New Hampshire

Mother Goddess

The mother goddess sits
in her garden throne
frogs and insects garnish her green skin she is deep deep deep
of the earth

the eyes of the sun rotate through her awareness the lord of
love sensuously caresses her tender breasts she sighs in
pleasure as her children partake of her beauty

moon drops are her ovaries
giving birth to all life

she rolls in her sleep
making mountains

the thunder is her singing
the lightning her insight

her tears wash away all sorrows
and her milk is the river of compassion and creativity

the ocean is her womb
and the earthquakes are her orgasms

she is beckoning us to follow
the path of the heart
which leads where she follows
to the light of the silvery dawn
in her eyes

Suzanne deVeuve
Cazadero, California

Prayer to Kali
(to be sung)

I am dying
While I'm living
I am so afraid
Help me, Kali
To die and be reborn

Dianne E. Jenett
Palo Alto, California

It's the Women
Pleadings to Ọṣún and the Divine Odù Ọ̀ṣẹ́ Méjì

On my knees
Breasts in hands
I beg you Ọṣún
Beat your ṣẹ̀kẹ̀rẹ̀
Gyrate your hips
Loose your song
Gather us
Long long rope
In the rhythm of your harmony

It's the women that make me
It's the women that break me

I have been revived absolute
in the deft hands of women I love
Honeyed fingers
Knead me back
to ancient belongings
Nullifying fragmentation

Cool water tongues
Incantate me

Wide and spacious
Light reflecting amber
Unbreakable and limitless

On my knees
Breasts in hands
I beg you Ọṣún
Beat your ṣèkèrè
Gyrate your hips
Loose your song
Gather us
Long long rope
In the rhythm of your harmony

It's the women that make me
It's the women that break me

I am spellbound
by the seductive nectar
of the heartbreaker promise
The pact of sisterhood
made around the kitchen table
Nestled in warm tortillas
Annointed with melting butter on hot cornbread
Invigorated by sambar soaked naan

Bound by sweet stickied cassava pone
And renewed with the passing
of the favored brick oven baked loaf

Very little talk is taboo
at the kitchen table
Perhaps more should be
As tongues easily muscle to
ridicule, condemn, annihilate
that "She" who is not of us
That She who may have once risen
from her laughter warmed chair
At this very table

There are kitchens
I am afraid to enter
That I might hear the walls
Now echoing my name
Scented with venom from mouths
That iterate stories and
Order the architecture
For my dispossession

On my knees
Breasts in hands

I beg you Ọṣún
Beat your ṣèkèrè
Gyrate your hips
Loose your song
Gather us
Long long rope
In the rhythm of your harmony

It's the women that make me
It's the women that break me

The stick we use to measure one another
has sharp and bloodied edges
with ever changing requisites for
The approvals and admittances

How adept we are
In fits of terror fueled rage
Siezing this stick and
Thrusting like master swordsman
Never missing the mark

We know her cracks
and breaking points
As she knows ours

As we collapse
on unyielding pavement
We gasp in the clutches
of broken covenants
and violated taboos
We grope validity
Spilling eloquent pleas
for buttressed righteousness
Coagulating our ruptures

On my knees
Breasts in hands
I beg you Ọṣún
Beat your ṣèkèrè
Gyrate your hips
Loose your song
Gather us
Long long rope
In the rhythm of your harmony

It's the women that make me
It's the women that break me

The thick skin I have been
unable to fabricate

I pray is a fortunate failure
Giving way to cyclical sheddings
and iridescent permeability
Tempered flesh drumming
Diastole
Systole
Breath in
Breath out

The making often requires
The breaking

Recurrent scraping
Collecting and injesting
my pieces and bits
I reconstitute myself
The labor of growing round
In sweetness

Like the honey bee to flower
I will return
To the kitchen table

I vow to corral
Bloodthirsty fears

So that I do not
Sting to my own death
already trampled blossoms

I would rather my hungers
Inspire the flowerings

On my knees
Breasts in hands
I beg you Ọṣún
Beat your ṣẹ̀kẹ̀rẹ̀
Gyrate your hips
Loose your song
Gather us, long long rope
In the rhythm of your harmony

It's the women that make me
It's the women that break me

Ìyámi Ọṣún
Forgive me for bleeding
the women I have loved
and those women I have not loved
They are all your beloved

River my memory
Power my word
Compassion my acts
with the knowledge that
I am no more favored by you
than the women I fear as enemy
And still, precious
Beyond all beliefs
And beyond any terror

On my knees
Breasts in hands
I beg you Ọṣún
Beat your ṣẹ̀kẹ̀rẹ̀
Gyrate your hips
Loose your song
Gather us, long long rope
In the rhythm of your harmony

It's the women

Xochipala Maes Valdez
Oakland, California

Dancing in Place

Oh Lady, Lady of the changing shapes
help me remember
how to dance in place;
when to witness,
when to harness,
when to charge with all my forces.

I don't know the reaches of my fate.
I know your shadow falls across my face.

Oh Lady, Lady of the Great Below.
Hard are your lessons,
many-fanged your harshness;
irresistible are your passions
and sweet, sweet are your praises.

I don't know the mazes of your soul.
I know your shadow falls beside me
everywhere I go.

Judy Grahn
Palo Alto, California

the shekhinah as mute

our mothers tremble vibrate
hesitate at the edge of speech
as at an unmade bed, their mouths work, confused

our mothers helpless to tell us
She whom you seek sacrificed
her place before the throne

dived into the atomic structure
of matter and hides there
hair wings streaming

womb compassionate pitiless
eyes seeing to the ends of the universe
in which life struggles and delights in life

they cannot take our hands show us
how to take comfort in raisins and apples
break apart laughing spit seed

they cannot say *seek me*
they teach us cooking clothing craftiness
they tell us their own stories of power and shame

and even if it is she who speaks through their mouths
and has crawled through ten thousand wombs until this day
we cannot listen

their words fall like spilled face powder

learn to recognize the gestures

when her hands cup her breasts
she enjoys her sweet strength
sap ascends the oak

dancing she causes
the young to dance
and to kiss

she may carry a weapon
a knife a gun a razor
she may wear a belt of skulls

when she discharges her anger in laughter
white lightning illuminates the horizon
from pole to pole

often she lays her hand over her eyes

like a secretary leaving
an office building at evening

cradling that infant boy
sitting him on her lap
smoothing the folds of her dress: this means pity

arms crossed: this signifies judgment

Alicia Ostriker
Princeton, New Jersey

. . .*for whom writing itself is spiritual practice, and whose mantra, when she needs to pray, is B'rucha at, shekhina.*

Conjurations for Healing

The following invocations were written for a healing ritual to help survivors of childhood sexual abuse. These invocations call forth the energy and power of the Yoruba female deities of the ocean, the wind and the sweet waters of the world to bring healing from the traumas women may have suffered from this malady.

Yemaya, Dream Creator, Full Moon Mama, Isis of the Veil, we come asking you to open the path to your knowledgeable watery depths to help Enduring Woman find within herself the knowledge and peace she needs to complete this work today. Take her into your nurturing arms and wash her clean of the disrespect borne by her body as you soothe the little girl within.

Empress of the Storm, Lightning Mother, Divine Warrioress, Oya, send your cleansing wind to change this life of pain to one of known courage. Help Enduring Woman to blow away the shadowy abusive remembrances of childhood that plague her mind and keep her from living a fulfilling life. Bring your transmuting power as a gentle breeze that cools and calms while relieving her inner torment.

Oshun, Keeper of the Sweet Rivers of Life, Sensuality Queen, Passionate Love Weaver, Beauty's Light in the World, let your spicy nectar flow through Enduring Woman and cleanse her female organs of any violence or trauma they have suffered. Bathe her in your abundant golden sweetness and light to bring new feelings of joy to replace her tears of woe.

We thank you gracious divinities for these blessings which you bestow upon Enduring Woman today. Ache'

Uzuri Amini
Oakland, California

Of Flames and Ashes

I am a woman of possibilities;
And I dance at the edge of the sands.

I am a woman of flames:
Of flames
And of ashes.

The sun knows me.
The sky sees me.
The sea: it sings
A slow deep call to prayer.

My bones—composed
From dust of long dead stars—
Sing with it.

Dust
Returns to flame, and flesh
Translates to light.

The Sun does not consume me.

I am transfigured.

Jan Jobling
Liverpool, England

A Devotee's Prayer

I invoke the five-fold blessing of the Lady of Healing

May I be blessed with health
May I be blessed with wealth
May I be blessed with love
May I be blessed with creativity
May I be blessed with wisdom

May I see with your vision
May I heal with your touch
May I walk with your clarity
May I dance with your grace
May I know with your heart
May I shine with your radiance

And may those I love be blessed and healed
Transformed and protected
And led in service to the world's healing.

Bless me Mother for I am your child
Bless me Mother for I am your child
Bless me Mother for I am your child

Arisika Razak
San Francisco Bay Area

Praise Song to the Goddess Mūkāmbikā

This praise song is for Goddess *Mūkāmbikā*. The Hindu tradition believes in a single formless being as the creator of the universe. The creator is not separate from creation. In fact, the creator is the creation, is manifest as the creation in the form of the elements, the forces of nature, the immutable laws, and as the witness, the all-pervasive sentience that is present in the body-mind-sense complex. Therefore, in the Hindu cosmology, everything is sacred, and non-separate from the whole. One can invoke "God" in any form or function, or in any gender. Mother Goddess worship in India is extremely popular, and has a long and rich history.

The word "Ambikā" means mother, and "Mūkā" means mute. "*Mūkāmbikā*" therefore means, "the Goddess who renders harmful desires mute." This explanation is derived from an ancient legend where a demon by the name *Kāmhāsura* prayed for the boon of immortality. However, when the time came to ask for this boon, the Goddess sat on *Kāmhāsura's* tongue, rendering his desire speechless. In preventing the demon from voicing his desire, the Goddess saved all beings from being infinitely subjected to his terror.

The Hindu philosophy does not have the concept of a devil as a parallel reality to God. The demons, which appear in the stories of the *Purāna* (mythological texts), are allegorical representations of the shadow side of individuals. Demons are often portrayed as beings with strong desires for domination and immortality. In fact, in most cases, demons are just devotees gone astray.

We need the grace of the creator to overcome the obstacles posed by the mind, in the form of habitual orientations and desires that lead one away from one's sense of being and purpose. One does not have the power to control one's thoughts and fancies as they arise in the mind. However, one can cultivate the discrimination to distinguish between the thoughts and fancies one can pursue and those that one should let go. Surrendering to the Great Mother, the source of everything—including one's thoughts and fancies—one gains inner space, a growing sense of resolution and clarity.

This song to the Mother Goddess *Mūkāmbikā* eulogizes her as an incarnation of the knowledge of oneself as limitless, and free of all longing. The Goddess protects those who surrender to her. She is the essence of OM, the contemplation of which relieves one from the bonds of sorrow. She bestows discrimination, and the ability to let go, and composure, in the form of a mind that is unbridled by conflict and therefore capable of grasping the message of its wholeness and glory. The Goddess *Mūkāmbikā* is formless and beyond all divisions; she is indeed the knowledge born of the Veda. Where does this glorious Goddess reside? She shines in the cave of one's own heart.

Praise Song for Goddess Mūkāmbikā

Rāga (melody) Kalvātī   *Tāla (rhythm) Khaṇḍa Cāpu*

ध्यायामि मूकाम्बिकां जगदम्बां ध्यायामि मूकाम्बिकाम् ॥

dhyāyāmi mūkāmbikāṃ jagadambāṃ dhyāyāmi
mūkāmbikām

I contemplate upon Goddess Mūkāmbikā, mother of the
universe. I contemplate on Goddess Mūkāmbikā.

प्रज्ञानघनरूपिणीं प्रणतकलुषनिवारिणीम् ।
प्रकृतिपाशविमोचिनीं प्रणवात्मिकाम् ॥

prajnānaghanarūpiṇīṃ praṇatakalauṣanivāriṇīṃ
prakrtipaśavimochinīṃ praṇavātmikām

Presiding in the form of pure consciousness, remover of
afflictions for those who surrender, freer of the bonds of
illusion, whose form is the sacred om

ध्यायामि मूकाम्बिकां जगदम्बां ध्यायामि मूकाम्बिकाम् ॥

dhyāyāmi mūkāmbikāṃ jagadambāṃ dhyāyāmi
mūkāmbikām

I contemplate upon Goddess Mūkāmbikā, mother of the
universe, I contemplate on Goddess Mūkāmbikā

विवेकवैराग्यवरदां शमादिसम्पदायुताम् ।
निष्कलां निगामान्तजां निजगुहचराम् ॥

Vivekavairagyavaradāṃ śamādisampadāyutāṃ
Niṣkalāṃ nigamāntajāṃ nijaguhacarām
Bestower of discrimination and objectivity, endowed with the
treasures of composure and calmness.
Her nature is beyond all division, understood through (the
study of) Vedanta; she shimmers in the cave of my heart

ध्यायामि मूकाम्बिकां जगदम्बां ध्यायामि मूकाम्बिकाम् ॥
dhyāyāmi mūkāmbikāṃ jagadambāṃ dhyāyāmi
mūkāmbikām
I contemplate upon Goddess Mūkāmbikā,
mother of the universe, I contemplate on Goddess Mūkāmbikā

Sadhvi Vrnda Chaitanya
Pavo, Georgia

A Prayer for Mealtime

O Great Mother, who bestows abundance upon us.
We thank you for the living things
    (name the things you are eating)
  that have sacrificed their lives to nourish us.
We take this offering into our bodies that we may be strong.
Make us strong, Abundant Mother, that we may be able to
Replenish the earth.

Chief Luisah Teish
Oakland, California

Tribute to our Iyas

Iyas,

Goddesses, the mothers of our origin, we continually
   thank you, for your nurturing love and embraces.
Your energy and attributes reside within us throughout
   the universe.

Mother of fishes
Mother of us all
When I enter your waters, I turn to enter with respect
   to greet you
Touch your water
Touch my ori
To you mother, I speak my inner most emotions and dilemmas
To you my mother, you are the one who with your waves, wash
   away my pain, tears and troubles out into the expanse of
   your waters
Mother who washes me clean with her original salt bath
Mother who cares for her daughter's and sister's children as if
   they were her own
Ogun River in the old world, ocean waters in the new world
Mother of fishes
Mother of us all

Sweet scent of honeysuckle permeates the path entering
   your grove
Your grove of many winding and hidden paths
Monkeys chatter in treetops above the slow moving river
Slow flowing river that changes with the seasons
Figure with outstretched arms waits to greet all who arrive in
   memory of ancient times
Mother's healing medicinal water
Osun River
Warrior woman who saved her city from intruders
   single-handed
Woman who received secrets of Ifa as a gift
Owner of brass shining like gold
Sweet woman
Beautiful woman
The sun retreats underneath the clouds, buckets of rain
   resemble glistening silver pellets shower the devout,
   leaving the grove
We welcome your blessing
We thank you for your sweetness to sweeten our lives
Your praises are numerous

Mother of nine
Warrior bush cow woman, with copper bangles

Swirls with the wind sweeping up and commanding change
   desirable or undesirable

One who gains access to ancestral portals
Dances with cow whisks
Mother of Niger River
Sweeping money with her broom
Eepa Heyi !
What a goddess !

Iyanifa Fasina (Sheila Carr)
Staunton, Virginia

O Sarasvati: request to grant inspired thought

for "dhi" as inspired thought which leads to Sarasvati-Vac of
    speech and knowledge
dhi as
thought
wisdom
poetic vision
poetic thought
intuition
sarasvati is the ultimate wealth for poets
may we receive dhi directly from Her

Pure Sarasvati, rich in rewards,
who finds goods through inspired thought, longs for our offerings
Sarasvati has received the offering.

Sarasvati reveals herself as mighty flood, that is how She reveals
She directs all inspired thought.

O Sarasvati, lead us to prosperity.
May you not push aside. May you not fail us with your flow.

Malgorzata Kruszewska
Russian River, Northern California

To the Earth and Birth Goddess

To the Earth and Birth Goddess

and to Ariadne with your thread,
my name sake and re-membrance,

To you who hovers above
below
around
and within me,
guiding my initiation into motherhood and its blood mysteries.

May I remember you

may I know you and feel you

may I heal what has been left asunder in my telling of you

may my stories ring out the praises of you

may this thesis do justice to you

Holy One I stand with my palms opened to you
I am grateful for these gifts of love,

for the children at my feet
for the love and play and

effort of getting them here.

Your voice strains to be heard within me,
I bow before you
offering myself over
and over
and over

     to your call.

Nané Ariadne Jordan
Vancouver, British Columbia

Blessing for the Birth of a New Baby Girl

May your heart grow larger and more open.
May you hear her feet on your floor and her voice in your ears.
May she stretch you and make you soft.
May she tickle you and make you round.
May she challenge you and make you strong.
May she love you as much as you do her.
May you remind her that she comes from the Goddess.
May you reassure her that she will return.
May you be the face of the Goddess for one another always.

Kate Wolf-Pizor
Mountain View, California

Homage to Her

As daughter, sister, lover, mother, wife
I've walked in every shoe,
worn every hat.
Who best to guide me through this varied life?
Who best to hold my hand through all of that?
I don't want strong reproach or wrath
Spare me the firm judgmental rod
She gently leads me on my path
I simply can't relate to God.

Kaye Schuman
New Jersey, 2009

Song for the Evening Star and the Morning Star

I greet Her as She ascends above
I greet Her as She floods the skies with light
I greet the first daughter of the Moon,
Star of Her Mother's Womb
I greet the Sacred Cow, crowned with crescent horns
I greet the Queen of the Date Palm

I sing as you ascend
I sing your praises

I stand before you in reverence
I bow before you who rides the lion
The power of the untrod mountain
I bow before you who holds the bird
The essence of the underground streams
I bow before the Queen of Earth Tree Sky

I sing your praises as the people parade with silver bells
I sing as the holy drums beat for you
I sing as you ascend in radiance, in exalted dignity

I offer you honey-paste and date-cakes
I offer barley beer and red wine

I offer the seven fruits
I offer cedar leaves and incense
I offer my new moon blood
I offer my pleasure
I offer song

Inanna, Ishtar, Ashera, Isha-S'tar, Shulamit, to praise you is
    sweet!
To pour libations, perform purification rites, heap up incense
    offerings, to burn juniper, to set out food offerings, to set
    out offering bowls.
To honor the Divine Lady is sweet! To celebrate Her
    abundance is sweet!
You are the Mistress born with Earth and Sky, joy of the
    people, ornament of the assembly, Lady of the Evening,
    Lady of the Morning,
You are mighty, you are respected, you are exalted, you are
    ever new,
and your praise is good.

The Lady exalted high as heaven ascends!
The Lady exalted as heaven smiles to us!
The Lady exalted high as heaven
Her greatness spans the borders of the universe!

The Lady ascending watches over us,
May we behold your beauty daily.

D'vora K'lilah, 2008
San Francisco, California

A prayer for Afrika

God our Goddess
creator of all and our Ancestors
We thank you for this gift of life
We accept with humility
opportunities to give and receive love
We accept with gratitude
the sacred gift of self-love
Deliver us from a burden of self-pity
Let us not be buried in a heap of self-hate
Help us go through the darkness
to make room for the light
Teach us to be teachers
Help us to be learners
May we stay remarkable
full of hope and laughter
May we also accept moments of grief
as a reminder of the duality of life
Help us share our soul with the world
without comprising our identity
Let us be reminded
that we are the world and that
if we truly believe
in our wisdom, so will the world

We accept dear Goddess
the gift of being chosen as midwives
for Africa's rebirth
May we be guided dear Ancestors
as we emerge from spiritual slavery

We welcome
the presence of the intangible
in our daily lives
Through the grace of Him in Her
May Africa in all of us
blossom for ever more.

Amen

Mmatshilo Motsei
South Africa

Wudu—Ablutions

Purifying the heart with water and light
We receive peace in all humility
Purifying the mind with water and light
We receive forgiveness that is beauty
Purifying the body with water and light
We receive patience and endurance.
Love washes
Releasing us from bondage
Allowing surrender into the ocean of Unity.
This skin of Light, now brightness woven

Murshid Mariam Baker
Fairfax, California

---

*Wudu is the act of cleansing the body to prepare for union with the Beloved in prayer.

Call of the Mermaid

Mami Wata, Yemoja, Erzulie, Lorelei, Nyai Roro Kidul~~~
I hear your Song

Mermaids, Sirens, Undines and Water Nymphs~ these enchant-
ing and powerful aquatic females have long held a deep fas-
cination for me. Goddesses of rivers, lakes, ponds, brooks,
oceans and seas, these water spirits are elemental forces
who help us surrender to the irresistible calls from the
depths of our psyches. The Mermaid guides us to remember
our sacred power and passions. She governs our dreams and
leaves mythical imprints on our psyches. She inspires us in
song, dance, and poetry. She helps us purify and balance our
bodies, hearts and minds. She swims in our tears. She floats
in our laughter.

She beckons us into a world of emotional depth, transformation, and magic.

She is sexual. She is sensual. She is flirtatious and dazzling.

She teaches us the secrets of seduction, irresistible charm and
unwavering allure. She embodies a powerful brilliance and
magnetism.

She is the Mysterious Power of the Unknown.

The Mermaid knows her Self.

She is the *Meerjungfrau*, the Ocean Virgin, Whole unto Herself. She is a Goddess of Radiant Beauty and Immanent Power that cannot be reckoned with...

Laura Amazzone
Los Angeles and San Francisco

The Bearers Of The New Day's Dawn

Fire will not burn me
Flames cannot consume me
I am the bearer of the new days dawn

Draw closer to my flames
Listen, and hear my names *
Learn my stories
Put them forth
My memories to survive

From the darkness to the light
In the dawn i will take flight
I am here
And the magic is alive

Fire will not burn us
Flames cannot consume us
We are the bearers of the new days dawn

Draw closer to our flames

---

*Here is where the chorus begins to softly but audibly intone the names of those persecuted as heretics, heathens and witches. The voices fade to a hum as they repeat the names to the end of the song.

Listen, and hear our names *
Learn our stories
Put them forth
Our memories to survive

From the darkness to the light
In the dawn we will take flight
We are here
And the magic is alive

Patti Davis
San Francisco, California

*Here is where the chorus begins to softly but audibly intone the names of those persecuted as heretics, heathens and witches. The voices fade to a hum as they repeat the names to the end of the song.

The snake, the tree

The snake whispers into Eve's ear from the Tree of Knowledge,
the snake that is rightly her own
   coiled,
making ready to unleash the babe within,
   the apple the fruit of her own desire.
High Holy Tree of Knowledge!
may I know you,
and know you
and know you again

your fruit feeds the fruit of my own womb.

Nané Ariadne Jordan
Vancouver, British Columbia

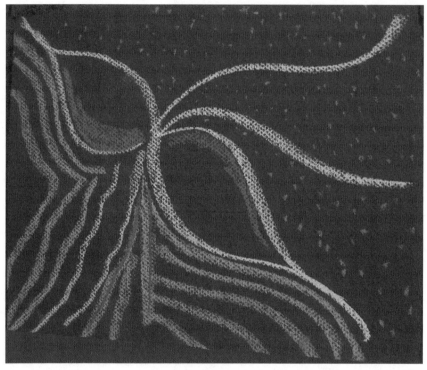

As the Sea Sees by Luisah Teish

Invocation in Remembrance of Female Originators

We invoke you, Mother of Deities: Neith, Akka, Teteoinan
Anu, Nana Bulukú, Kybele who is Mater Deum, and Dôn
Limitless Aditi, Hannahanna, Athirat—Qaniyatu Elima—
Old Woman in the Moon, Nyame the sole procreatrix

Mother Creator Ngalyod, Kunapipi and Mutjingga
Each named Mother of Us All, and also Terra Ops
She serpents, eternal: Amaná who has borne all beings,
And mighty old Mother Tiamat, who bore them all

Nammu, who gave birth to heaven and earth, and
Above the abyss formed people out of clay—Nü Gua too—
Mummu, the creatrix of heaven and earth, who directs;
Great Aruru, Mother Hubur, who fashions all things
Firm are your decrees, past withstanding are they

Our Grandmother Kokomtheyna who created everything
And Ja Pudeu, who brought it all into being by blowing,
Nana Dumat, and Our Mother Gaucheováng, who is aluna, the
vast Waters who originated the nine worlds: everything

Ts'its'tcs'inako, whose mind creates reality in space,
She-Spider, also called Kokyangwuhti—and Weaver, and

Grandmother, and Fire-Bringer. Ix Chebel Yax who journeys
The night skies, crossing your loomsticks to ward off jaguars

O Spinning Woman, Seventh Nummo, you who set the sun
Rolling in space like a drop spindle, whirled by a copper spiral
O great Calabash who are the female Origin of Being
You the Chalice, you the Basket, you the Cauldron

Wyrd who is mightiest, fate-weaver who goeth as she shall,
And the all-wise Moirae, Parcae, Norns: Three Sisters
Who travel over the Sea of Age in deep foreknowing
O ancient ones, you shape the passing year-days

Sekhmet with your Tablets of Destiny, Seven Hathors of birth,
Auset the Great Enchantress, Life-Giver of Ten Thousand
    Names
Atete who governs the fates of people, who looks after us
Fortuna, Tyche, Nemesis, and the Eumenides

Uludun-mama, who created heaven and earth,
Aoyazun who birthed all living beings, Omosi-mama
Our Great Grandmother Nakawe, who creates growth,
And you Three Grandmothers who guard the Waters
Under the great stone pillar of Heaven and Earth.

O primal Tao, creating Mother of whatever exists under the sky
Upon whom myriads of beings depend for their birth and
    existence
Xi Wang Mu, Old Tigress, Original Breath of the Great Yin
No one knows your beginning, and no one knows your end

Max Dashú
Oakland, California

Why We Drum

Native/American Indian women wonder above all others how it has come to be said, let alone believed and enforced, "Women don't sit at the drum." Mother Earth herself is a drum and heartbeat of all people. All life upon her lives in her universal rhythm, her songs being a language of universal 'vibrations' that are nature's patterns. Life cycles, from sky to water and animal to stone, observe complex cycles and patterns that may be heard and felt in the basic rhythm of the drum. More than any other instrument used to create music, the drum elicits and expresses more human emotion in its song than any other. Whatever the emotion, there exists a drum rhythm to match and please the feeling. Vibrations of the drum themselves are dynamic and resilient, sensual and powerful—mirroring the spirit of Native women. It is as natural for a woman to sit at the drum and lift her voice as it is for tides to resonate vibrations of water and earth, and when she sits and sings, the drum becomes a physical extension of a woman's spiritual expression to create music.

As human beings we each come from a woman, to be nurtured by a woman, and continue to suck off of a Woman - Mother Earth—throughout our life. Her heartbeat is the music of a woman's song. Not the music heard from the physical and mechanistic style of a man, equally important to balance in our world, but emotional and melodic. As with giving, nurturing, guiding and keeping life, women accept the responsibility of that heartbeat song and are now claiming a place at the drum with hearts that resonate healing. Native women have an ancient story to sing and tell, beginning with the heartbeat of creation and continuing through the medicine of the drum. It may be more correct to ask, "Why *don't* women sit at the drum?"

April Lea Go Forth
Modoc County, California,
at the Oregon border

Harvest Blessing

I bless this harvest gathering in the name of the Morrigan who is the Dark Mother, who comes to us in our brokenness and our need for change.

Breathe and know that She is the Great Transformer.

After harvest comes rest and regeneration. Darkness is preparation for the rebirth of the Light; and so the dance of life continues from cycle to cycle.

Oh Great Dark Mother, gather our brokenness, our doneness, our fatigue and disappointment. Cover us with the nurturing darkness. In the nurturing darkness, may we believe in and dream of the light.

May you be held in the knowledge that all manner of things shall be well and that, no matter what, they shall change.

Blessed Be

Kate Wolf-Pizor, 2008
Mountain View, California

Namo Guan Shih Yin Pusa
I call upon-take refuge in/look/world/sound/bodhisattva
"I call upon the Bodhisattva who sees and hears
the cries of the world"

Bowing, calling, honoring...praising, taking refuge in
Guan Yin, Bodhisattva of Awakening

Namo Guan Shih Yin pusa, namo Guan Shih Yin pusa
Namo Guan Shih Yin pusa, namo Guan Shih Yin pusa

Calling on Guan Yin, Mother of Compassion
Calling on Guan Yin, Goddess of Mercy and Kindness
Calling on Guan Yin, Mother of Protection
Calling on Guan Yin, Goddess of Forgiveness

Namo Guan Shih Yin pusa, namo Guan Shih Yin pusa
Namo Guan Shih Yin pusa, namo Guan Shih Yin pusa

Taking refuge in Guan Yin,
She who hears the cries of her children
Taking refuge in Guan Yin,
She who sees and eases all suffering
Taking refuge in Guan Yin,
She who pours sweet nectar of healing

Taking refuge in Guan Yin,
She who opens the way to free all beings

Bowing, calling, honoring...Praising, taking refuge in
Guan Yin, Bodhisattva of Awakening

Music and Lyrics by
Evelie Delfino Sáles Posch (c) 2005
El Cerrito, California

Shekinah War Poems

1. Full Moon

Where does My soul Bird Build Her Nest
what heavens kiss her wings in flight
Y La Luna Llena
emblazoned in the starry night
whispers her silence.

2. ADAMAH

red earth and clay
iron and ancient blood
La mesa spreads thin against the twilight
Old ones poke at fire
bake mythology into bread
children enchanted by stories
let loose
secrets held down by day
coyote grins
plots her evening adventure
fools herself into believing
rabbit is easy prey

coyote hunts with no borders
but her own imagination

Remember says an old one
where no child knows night sky
or fire
or story
coyote chews her own tail

3. Hiroshima Conversation

Bodies
printed on stone
carbon silhouettes
half the mountain in ash
Mrs Takeyda's story
contains nothing familiar
such as
how her parents met at a high school dance
her story begins
after the apocalypse
charred remains
mouth burn
lip burn
eye lid torn

bleeding all over
skin hanging down
no words

people in the river
float away
not knowing i am a broken stalk
i struggle to say my name

4. iraq

what words
comfort a woman
whose home is in ruins
whose children are dead
do you tell her
cover your mirrors
walk bare foot in the ruins
rip your clothing near your heart
my heart is a shroud
my eyes are tombs
my mouth a grave
i sit alone
i cry alone
trees gone

animals gone
birds gone
the earth has become dust
the rivers run with blood
bombs fall from the sky
what will become of us
what will become of us
what will become of us

5. After 911

Five oclock in the afternoon
Abdul Rauf, Ibrihim and I
head east toward the subway
having walked a long walk
a pilgrimage walk
on the island of manhattan
from the site of an algonquin village
to ground zero
following broadway
financial district, garment district
times square
upper west side
to bnai jeshurun
continuing along broadway

on to 125th street
across harlem
back down lenox
to the mosque of malcolm x
september 11, 2003
abdul rauf and i
carrying a sign that says
to save one life is to save the entire world
we are a muslim jewish peacewalk pilgrimage
making a statement
by our presence together.
The buddhist monks from japan
who accompany us
and know from previous experience
just where to stop and find bowel relief, water
and a beautiful place for lunch,
all in the public realm
we walk two by two
so we don't need permits
to say peace is possible
abdul rauf and i carry a banner
'to save one life is to save the world entire'
Torah and Quran
all along the way
people stopped and stared

read our banner
looked confused
and to a person
smiled, clapped, cheered, walked along with us
for a while
at the end of the day
when my legs questioned every step
abdul rauf, brother ibrihim and i walk up to a Muslim brother
sitting
on a beach chair
behind a rickety table
he is selling incense, religious trinkets
music tapes and five and ten cent wares
his face porous like basalt
harbors one eye glazed with blindness
asalaam aleykum brother
ualeykum salaam
we exchange conversation
how are you brother what is your story
he says
i am survivor of attica
was there during the uprising
saw brothers shot dead
personally withstood the blows
still feel the crushing weight

of white America
who withholds resources from the poor
and gives it to the war
imprisons male children of ex-slaves
turns their mothers into maids
makes hardly any effort
to use taxpayer money
to turn broken neighborhoods
into a land of milk and honey
i like what you're about he says
i approve of this walk
we all need to walk
neighborhood by neighborhood
street by street
until dignity is restored
work is plentiful
healthcare is everywhere
and children are not shot in the streets
go in peace he says
go in peace

Rabbi Lynn Gottlieb
Berkeley, California

Ohlone Hummingbird Blessing

One day, a Mayan elder called me up to say she had had a dream that she felt she need to share with Ann Marie Sayers, Tribal Chairwoman, Indian Canyon, Mutsun Ohlone. She said the message involved Ohlone women, and asked if I'd drive her out. I promised we'd go out to Gilroy as soon as the weekend came. We agreed on the date and time before hanging up.

I remained curious the rest of the week, yet, I felt a blessing to be part of sharing the message. Only months before, I had been invited to an environmental conference held in Baja California. An elder woman from the Kumeyaay (Diegueno) Nation blessed the launch of what was a promising weekend of discussions, networking and bonding over environmental issues.

The elder lit sage, not the copal I was most used to smelling when at ceremonies in Mexico. I was struck since we also use sage in California. I was even more moved when later the Kumeyaay women showed me their regalia, the skirts worn by their dancers, which looked much like the skirts of the Ohlone, and like the skirt I had made in preparation over a year for a special honoring for Ohlone elder women.

Ann Marie allowed me to participate, even though my research for my family genealogy and journey to confirmation that we were Ohlone had just begun. I could not say why I spoke up and asked to be a part of the circle, little did I know I'd learn some of the most valuable lessons.

Over that year, I gathered once a month with Ohlone women as we learned how to make our regalia, as we were taught to pray with each shell that went on our necklaces. Every shell we stung on the sinew represented a prayer for the community, for the elders, for our environment, for the women, for our next generations. Thousands of prayers were said that year.

Yet, an even larger gift awaited us all. Friendship.

Over plates of food, designs for skirts and headdresses, and bleeding pricked fingers, us women shared our life stories. We shared when we felt like it, laughed when we wanted, cried when we had to, and with each meeting, we came to know each other better. Not all our stories were pretty, in fact, often, we learned the most intimate of tales about mistakes, losses, lack, unsatisfied dreams.

The young ones kept us strong, and made us see that we needed a better future for ourselves, as women, as a community, as a nation.

When the elders saw us dance in their honor, smiles and tears and hugs were what greeted us when we finished. I truly have never felt such blessings and such honoring among women. That day we honored our elder women, for their sacrifices of culture and language and being when it was most dangerous to even admit being Native American. We honored each other, the women that sat around the table over that year, to recognize each woman's beauty, humanity and loving nature as survivors who were often raised by a generation who received the impact of early policies towards Native Americans: parents unable to express emotions, or unable to even, at times, to respect or honor each other, many refused to acknowledge again being Indian. In honoring the young women, I saw hope and a brighter horizon for which to fight today.

So, when I saw the Kumeyaay elder blessing with sage that day in Baja California, I suddenly saw the line that connects all women.

While we women had toiled in preparation for the elder ceremony, the waterfall at Indian Canyon had run very dry, only a trickle where before there had been a luscious sound of water falling the feet from the large rock above down into the pool below. At the environmental conference, I heard about Indigenous communities in Baja California with only contaminated water sources with which to quench the thirst of their children.

When the elder Kumeyaay woman asked me to join her in closing the environmental conference with prayer, I felt a huge honoring to be connecting the Ohlone and Kumeyaay in prayer for Water. I made a promise there in Baja that I would devote my prayer for the water. The Ohlone sent water with the Hopi who carried water to the large gathering in Mexico City in worldwide prayer for Water.

Dona Mary and I rumbled along the dirt road, passing the green rows of the vineyards, before giving way to rolling golden hills. We listened to music, each of us lost in thought, the warm sunny weather lulling our pores to breathe and take in the majesty that is the California landscape.

Later, inside Ann Marie Sayer's home, Dona Mary shared the dream that had come to her, and the importance of a gathering of Ohlone women in prayer for the environment, for water. We all spoke about the possibility yet no one knew the when or how or even if such a gathering could be pulled off. The wheels were set in motion.

In the time that passed after that meeting, I was visited constantly at my window by hummingbirds. It didn't matter what window I stood or sat near, eventually, a hummingbird would arrive and begin singing. I listened, day after day, until one day, I heard 1000 women dancing on the land of the Ohlone, a thousand women who would come together as we had in creating the honoring ceremony, to share our lives – our successes and failures, a place where women came together without judgment in support of each woman's process. A place where we didn't blame each other, gossip, cause each other pain in competition, instead, a place where we left all those characteristics at the door.

As Ann Marie says to those coming to Indian Canyon, 'leave your burdens in the basket by the entrance. They'll be there if you still want to pick them up on your way out.'

The blessings I hope for the 1000 Hummingbirds Ceremony are invoked through the telling of this story. It is my honor to share how the 1000 Hummingbirds came to be, and how you can invoke the Hummingbirds wherever you are:

Treat your women elders with utmost respect, pay them back with service, and forgive their choices bound by place and time. Come together as women in prayer for Water. Treat each other with love. Always make a space in your ceremony for those friends, acquaintances, family or colleagues who may be experiencing tough times, poor health or economic challenges—don't judge, embrace them, bring them in, tell them its going to be ok. Remember the water in every prayer, blessing or ceremony.

'Women are the life givers, we must respect each of the women in our lives. We need Water to survive. Give thanks to the river, streams, oceans and pools of water that sustain us and give us life too.' *Tony Cerda, Tribal Chairman, Costanoan Carmel Rumsen Ohlone.*

Catherine Herrera
San Francisco, California

The Time of Dreaming
For Jennifer Berezan and Joan Marler

The year rolls towards darkness.
It is the time of dreaming.
I look for a message in the night sky,
    in the temple under the earth,
    in stones and in stories.

It comes in the forms of a shooting star,
    of the ancient rocks' embrace,
    of a voice in the cave's fire.

Oh, Dark Mother!
I have resisted you all of my life.
I am afraid of the dark,
    hate winter,
refuse to accept death.

I fell in love with the goddess of Spring,
with her flowers and simple joy.
Then she turned into the queen of the dead
and dragged me down into the underworld.
A cruel trick, I think.
Either that or fate.

The voice says:
"You are mine.
You gave yourself to Persephone,
And your heart swells in the presence of black Madonnas
Because they are my manifestations.
I am prior to all."

I have a Dark Mother who holds me and leads me.
She has promised to walk with me
Through life and into death.
I, who am enamored of the light,
Am welcomed into the darkness.

I will have to reframe my thoughts,
change my ways,
laugh with the tricksters.

It is the time of dreaming,
And I am home.

Maya Spector
Menlo Park, California

New Moon Blessing
To be said at Rosh Chodesh (New Moon):

Shekhinah, we come to you at this time of the moon's renewal,
to join you in regeneration and rebirth
to plant new seeds
to honor this time of *piya wiconi*—new beginnings.
As we embark on new projects and contemplate new
ways of being
help us to see ourselves and each other with new eyes
of appreciation and gratitude,
to remember to thank you, daily, for all our blessings.

Help us to reach our own fullness,
Even as we go inside,
in seclusion with Her
She Who is waiting for us
To discover divinity
in ourselves

D'vorah J. Grenn, March 1998
San Mateo, California

Moving Between the Worlds
(talking to Lady of Largest Heart)

Power surges from within my mountainous arms.

Her defaming hand crushes the mountain to garbage.

A wail fills my heart.

>   Mountains brought to garbage
>   putrid   teeming
>   cauldron of rot.

All I built up
  melted down
  melted down
  melted down
Dark garbage fermenting
Earth power transforming bone
        heart
            belly
Her power within me.

>   I am the mountain and the garbage.
>   I am the power of change.

Dark full power surging
massive energy
power before time
rising
sweeping over
dark deep trunked
mountain.

I AM THE MOUNTAIN AND THE GARBAGE.
I AM THE POWER OF CHANGE.

Louise Pare
Ashland, Oregon

Of Durga and Nepal

When I think of Nepal I remember the women who carry the spirit of mai and ajima, the mother and grandmother spirit: and who I experience as living embodiments of Goddess Durga in all her forms. These women, whose lives are by no means easy, remind me of my own love and devotion towards Goddess. Watching them pray and speak to Durga, Lakshmi, Saraswati, Kali, Vajrayogini, the Matrikas, Navdurgas and other countless goddesses affirms that what I am feeling is real, mysterious and profound. At each temple, at each road side shrine, at each stone that has been worshiped for thousands of years as Goddess throughout the Valley, I encountered women dressed in vibrant red hues—cherry, hibiscus, crimson, ruby, pomegranate. Women on their knees in prayer, their eyes closed in deep devotion, their lips trembling slightly as they ask for Her blessing. Women feeding the Goddess-offering rice, chapatis, lentil-based sweets, fruit, and coconut. Women honoring Her light with ghee lamp flames burning from cotton wicks the women themselves had grown and so carefully and mindfully twisted while sitting on a door step and chatting with their neighbor about life's trials and joys. Women waving incense and teaching their young daughters how to hold the incense sticks and wave them in a circular movement to please the goddess- the wisps of smoke wafting through the womblike inner sanctum filling the air with sandalwood and jasmine scents. Women carrying plates piled with orange and yellow marigolds and red hibiscus, tucking the blossoms into every available crevice of the goddess' majestic stone form, especially at her feet, and on her head. Women reciting the sacred texts, muttering chants (mantras), whispering their fears and desires to the Goddess of their heart. Women bowing their heads to the deity's wet and sticky red feet and breasts, goddess' now blood red body lovingly smeared with red vermilion powder and coconut milk by thousands of devotees.

Countless women young and old, light and dark-skinned, poor, middle-class, rich, Buddhist and Hindu—all pressing their red marked foreheads to the Goddess' brow, then feet—expressing their deep devotion and love and asking for Her grace.

JAI MAA!

Laura Amazzone
Los Angeles and San Francisco

Gratitude

"Gracious Goddess, Mighty Mother of us all,
Bringer of all fruitfulness.
I do thank Thee for the blessings in my life
   (at this point I generally insert specific 'gifts')
May I continue to be worthy of your gifts."
Blessed Be

Wren
Honolulu, Hawaii

Brigit, Brede, Bridie, Bride

Brigit, Brede, Bridie, Bride
Goddess of many names—and one
It is time for your annual return.
Each year I go to wait for you
At the holy well with water trickling and candles burning.
Amongst the trees I smell the night.
Sometimes from afar a sheep calls
Her lamb newly-born or soon to be so.

Brigit, Brede, Bridie, Bride
I softly call your name, and ask for your blessing.
I call for your love and your protection
Your healing, your wisdom, your nurturing.
I ask for you to be with me, in the good times and the bad
To fill my body and my spirit with your presence.

Brigit, Brede, Bridie, Bride
Come beautiful Goddess, return to me once again!
Fill my body, heart and soul with your love.
You come with the promise of Spring in the earth.
Come fill me with hope and newness and freshness!

Come heal my battered and shattered edges!
Come Goddess of all that is fresh and whole!
Come again!
Brigit, Brede, Bridie, Bride – welcome!

Cheryl Straffon
Cornwall, Britain

A Blessing...

May Women all be treated
as rare and holy flowers
Petals strong and fragile
rise up sacred powers
Giving
Giving
Life its very breath

Sarah Blogg
Melbourne, Australia

Drum Chant

Hear the drum beat out our heart beats
Watch the eagle soar
Feel the bones rise up around us,
They have walked these lands before

From the old we'll build a new world
Lending hearts and minds
Together we can feel the power
When the Goddess lives inside

When the Goddess burns inside

Julianne Reidy, 2007
San Francisco, California

Divine Conversation: A short look into the window of one woman's sacred sojourn... mine

Spirit in the Bayou...

I set my bag down and looked out at different world. The trees seemed bent with old hope and weighed down with their witness of time and dreams gone by. The sky was a different color blue, bright with bold hue and used up with the reflection of time. The clouds moved by with urgency that was unfamiliar. They moved quickly to get past the relentless uncompromising glare of the midday sun.

The sun owned the sky in Baton Rouge, Louisiana. This was the heat that raised cotton, cane and tobacco from the deep crevices of the earth. This was the heat that commanded trees to hang down and weep. It carried the threat of exposure and the imperative to seek cover. It spoke to my body on a cellular level, and it promised to heat the air that held me even while it was covered with clouds rushing to wet the earth. It was relentless and it was an invitation to a new chapter in my life.

I walked outside and drank in the beauty of the grounds. There were pristine buildings with views and balconies and there were trees that made a circle around me. The quiet was a container to hold the cacophony of sounds that fell down around me. The insects were loud, and the birds audacious.

Bright colors on swift wings rushed by me punctuating the next chapter.

I walked with a slight limp. My body was bruised and tired. My spirit was a small light in a tight corner of my soul. My thoughts hung like wet laundry on a line suspended on the lines of my conscious thought. Oh Lord... please help me. Where am I?

I left California running for my life, and desperate to escape it. To say it was out of any semblance of order is akin to using a white crayon on white paper. The color is missing. The hues and pigment of the chaos are unrecognized in the entourage of leftovers from my life. The white crayon draws a non-descript line ignoring the content of the misery that I lived and that I knew.

Time to fold, and time to go.

But as I limped through the heat, exploring the wet complexity of my new home, I knew that I was desperate. I knew that the old songs were over. The notes of discord were stuck noisily in my past like the disconnection in a broken verse, or a broken record.

I walked into the vortex of another life. I watched myself pass the buildings examining the structures, taking note of my physical effort willing myself to continue. Tears slipped down my face making traces and lines that indicated I was still living.

I listened to the raucous notes called out by insects I had gratefully, never seen. I heard them mark a new boundary for my life and a challenge for my healing. I limped past the acknowledgement of my physical shortcoming. I drank in my surrounding, taking it down like strong medicine. I needed it. There was a quiet in the middle of the surrounding noise. I walked into it, slipped into the middle and looked again at the day that held me. I felt the frank heat of the sun move quickly to rest behind white clouds surging and billowing into their new position of prominence. They moved past my memories and sailed into new territory. It was space marked careful, enter as you will. I gathered my strength around me like old-fashioned petticoats that hung down and dragged against the dirt floor of my past. I needed to pull them close and I needed to keep walking. My hope beat against my heart, fluttering and stammering like a wish on a windy day.

It is so difficult to look for something and not know what it is. This was my search for my Holy Grail. It was a monumental task. It was of mythic proportion and it included the ingredients of a folk tale. The problem was that I was living it. I was breathing through it and limping on the perimeter. This was going to be a hard climb... I had to get ready.

Still, there was no manual, and no predecessor. There was no teacher, guru, or preacher on hand to meet me and show me the way. I had to rely on the small light that managed to shine from the abandoned corner of my soul. I had to rest on the desire I felt to be held and healed in my spirit. This was my premise and my promise to myself.

I knew stories of my ancestors who left the curtain of the Deep South for California high ground. I knew the memories of my community who passed bits and pieces of history like chips in a bag when I was growing up. I saw the children in my neighborhood go to the fields in Central California to pick fruit in the summer. Their parents loading them into tired undependable vehicles stuffed with blankets, fried chicken, peanut butter and jelly and the hope of making money for school clothes. It was the behavior that belonged behind the old curtain but made its way north. I remember the stark misery of slaves in the field. Pulling cotton with bloodied hands and stooped backs, under the punishing heat, and the threat of the overseer. They ran when they could... They followed the north star... and when they landed north they waited for the south to leave them.

But I ran the opposite direction. I came looking for a slowdown. I came running because my heart was on fire. It had been burning for as long as I could remember.

Cheryl Dawson
Berkeley, California

Amulet of Allat by Max Dashu

from Global Heart

Memory became myth,
>Myth was forgotten,
>>Forgetting became practice,
>>>Practice replaced thought.
Language became ritual,
>Ritual created ceremony,
>>Ceremony became art,
>>>Art replaced insight.
Feeling became need,
>Need fed greed,
>>Greed became power,
>>>Power replaced compassion.
Body became shame,
>Shame found word,
>>Word became mind,
>>>Mind replaced wisdom.
Form became law,
>Law evoked religion,
>>Religion became politics,
>>>Politics replaced justice.

Life became people,
    People dominated beings,
        Beings became objects,
            Objects replaced spirit.
Earth became resource,
    Resource acquired value,
        Value became God,
            God replaced love.
She became angry and sad.
She wept for us.
And she weeps today,
her moaning, a buried murmur.

It is the palpitation of the cosmos,
The bursting of arteries too long compressed.
It is the uncontrolled pulse of her dark waters,
leaking into the clean linen of our lives.

For our neglect and abuse, she rages.

She breathes her disease into our lungs
with breath we do not smell,
giving us despair.

She speaks her rage into our ears
with a language we do not understand,
giving us confusion.
She sings her pain into our throats
with a melody we do not hear,
giving us melancholy.
She cries her grief into our wombs
through the children we cannot bear,
giving us loneliness.

She is trying to warn us

We think her pain is our enemy.
It is the unspoken grief of our own crimes.
We think her blood is revolting.
It is the blood on our own hands.
We think her cries are deafening.
They are the silent screams of the night,
waking us from deep sleep.

Anne Bluethenthal
San Francisco, California

from Unsing the Song

and it will be said

and it will be said

that crimes unhealed
fester into the next horror
that victim and perpetrator
are no longer distinguishable

and it will be said

and it will be said

that our lives depend
not on another death
not on another life
but on tending our collective survival

and it will be said

and it must be said

that we acknowledge this truth
that we taste this reality
that we shed necessary tears
that we wage appropriate healing

and it must be said

that woman's body continues
to describe the terrain of hatred

and it must be said

and it must be said

that women's blood
is thick in the street
that the cost of slaughter
lies sick in the womb of our daughters

and it must be said

that we must weep now
and wail loudly
and heal those children
and hold them to our own bodies
and never
turn
away
again

Anne Bluethenthal
San Francisco, California

Auður*

Auður, my Goddess, my sister
You who are the Paradox
Treasure in the Void
Creatress
weaver of Destiny, wielder of Death
mistress of Love
Vanadís

I thank you for this Land
for the mountains and the valleys
the vibrant greens of Summer days
and golden red Sunna at midnight
the subtle blues of Winter
with the silvery hue of Mána
shimmering on the morning snow
I thank you for the Flow in my life
for the Gift of being born from my mother's Womb

---

*Auður is an old Nordic/Icelandic word filled with magic. It remains in the language as a woman's name, as a male noun meaning riches/wealth/treasure, and as a male adjective meaning empty. Its meaning as a female noun used to be: destiny, death, happiness, fortune, goddess of fate, web of fate (Magnússon, Ásgeir Blöndal. 1989. Íslensk orðsifjabók. Reykjavík: Orðabók háskólans.)
Mána means Moon goddess.

and I thank you for receiving me into Your Eternal Womb
when this life ceases to be

I thank you for the bliss of bearing my daughter
from my womb into this world
I thank you for the softest touch
my grandson's cheek on mine
his song giving me hope
his laughter lightening up my soul
his tears touching the depths of my being
I thank you for the joy and the pain in my heart
For the loving and the longing
the tears and laughter
songs and silence

Auður
Teach me the Dance of the Dísir*
Help me spread my wings and fly
so that I may soar towards the Stars
Teach me to reach down
and touch the roots for re-membering
my ancient relations

*Dísir is an old Icelandic word for goddesses.

Teach me to find the strength in humility
accept and respect when I don't see
to weave my web
in harmony
with the Great Web of Life

Sister, teach me the Magic of your Song

Valgerður H. Bjarnadóttir
Iceland, 2009

Qadesha ("Sacred Whore")

The blood of Ishtar,
Goddess of Desire,
Flows through my body.

Isis forms my heart,
Her honey sweetens my vulva

Astarte moves my womb –
Wanting the hard phallus.
As the Tree of Life seeks the sky,
So my silken limbs entwine the tall king.

My lips are sweet. Life is in my mouth.
Beneath my robes—I am Glorious.

When I dance, the sun sails safely through the night.
When I dance, the future is formed by my feet.
When I dance, the stars move through the heavens.

When I dance, women perfume their thighs, drape gold upon
     their breasts.
When I dance, the maiden laughs and tosses her hair.
When I dance, the youth writes poetry, waits under the moon.

When I dance, the matron teases her husband—the husband
becomes generous.

When I dance, Venus shimmers the desert.
When I dance, dust becomes silver, stones are made of
gold.

Cosi Fabian
San Francisco, California

Queen of the Night

Queen of the night,
In twilight
Revealed Herself
אור יקרות שופע
Light!

Magnificent and plenty
Pours,
Like mountains of satin
In the sky
בואי אלי
פנימה

Let your magic fly
אמא,
בתוכי ומסביב לי
ותמיד
Flower into seed

אני כמהה אליך
אני מגיעה עדיך
אני יונקת משדיך
Queen
Of the Night...

Queen of the Night

Queen of the night,
In twilight
Revealed Herself
Orr yekarott shofeah,
Light!
Magnificent and plenty,
Pours
Like mountains of satin
In the sky
Bo'ee elai,
Pnimah,
Let your magic fly

Ee-mah,
B'To'chi, U-misaviv li,
V'Tamid,
Flower into seed
Ani kme'hah elaich,
Ani megi'aha elaich
Ani yoneket me'shadaich,
Queen
Of the Night...

DeAnna L'am
Hebrew-English, © 1996
Santa Rosa, California

O-yuki-san*
a prayer to diminish snowfall

O-yuki-san,
Turn your face away.
Do not comb out your long hair here.
Do not set the white flakes flying
To bar our way.

O-yuki-san,
Keep your kimono closed.
Be modest and demure.
Do not open your kimono here.
Do not show us your pale smooth body
Lest your beauty blind us.

O-yuki-san,
Fold up your ivory fan
And tuck it into your sleeve.
Do not hold it in your hand.
Do not fan it back and forth here
In front of your face

---

*Yuki-san is a Japanese spirit or goddess of the snow, also sometimes called Yuki-onna.

To stir the stern cold winds.
O-yuki-san,
Show us your mercy and not your glory.
Be compassionate to us here.
Wise and ancient spirit of the snow,
We honor you with saki and sweet rice balls.
We honor you with cuttings of paper
And with paper folded into cunning shapes.
Take our offerings and leave us in peace.

O-yuki-san, heed our prayer.

Elizabeth Barrette
Charleston, Illinois

Las Hijas De La Malinche
The Daughters Of La Malinche

A un español, Hernán Cortés,
que llamaban los aztecas Malinche,
tradujo una joven esclava, las flores de su lengua,
Malintzin, mujer indigena, fiel creyente de la virgen,
traductora del encuentro que transforma México,
lengua del Nuevo Mundo.
   - Lila Downs, from her CD "One Blood"

Morena, nuestra vida comenzó contigo
Las flores de tu lengua
Engendraron a la raza cósmica
Madre Nuestra, santificado sea tu nombre
Mujer violada que padeciste por tus hijas.

Marina, Malintzin, Malinalxochilt, madre nuestra
Venimos a honrarte, madre indigena de las mestizas.
Niña morena, nos parecemos tanto a ti
Somos del color de la tierra
Somos las hijas de la Malinche

Con honor aceptaste tu destino
Y por eso mereces nuestro respeto

Mujer llena de gracia y cabal
Que la historia no supo apreciar.

Somos tus hijas Malinche
Y nosotras te vamos a redimir
Por nuestra raza hablará el espíritu
Y los que te demonizaron lo pagaran.

Marina, Malintzin, Malinalxochilt, nuestra madre
Venimos a honrarte, madre indigena de las mestizas.
Niña morena, nos parecemos tanto a ti
Somos del color de la tierra
Somos las hijas de la Malinche

To a Spanish conqueror called Hernan Cortes,
whom the Aztecs called Malinche,
a young slave translated the flowers of her tongue,
Malintzin, native Indian woman, faithful religious
   believer,
translator of the encounter that transforms Mexico,
language of the New Time.
   - Lila Downs, from her CD "One Blood"

Dark-skinned woman, our life started with you
The flowers of your tongue engendered the cosmic race

Our mother, hallowed be thy name
Raped woman who suffered for her daughters.
Marina, Malintzin, Malinalxochitl, our mother
We come here to honor you, Indian mother of the Mestizas.
Dark-skinned little girl, we look just like you
We are like the Earth's color
We are the daughters of La Malinche.

You accepted with honor your fate
You deserve our respect
Woman full of grace and worthy
Whom history did not appreciate.

We are your daughters, Malinche
And we are going to redeem you.
Through our race, spirit will speak
And those who demonized your name will pay for it.

Marina, Malintzin, Malinalxochitl, our mother
We come here to honor you, Indian mother of the Mestizas.
Dark-skinned little girl, we look just like you
We are like the Earth's color
We are the daughters of La Malinche.

Aurora Medina
San Francisco Bay Area

Goddess Awake and Arisen

Goddess your blood red cape flowing with the waters of the
　　birth canals
Goddess your forehead raised to the rising sun's rays –
Dawn light flickering across a brow of flesh colored sandstone
Eyes glinting from the light of this day's creation

Your sight covered by sand for millennium, hands reach out to
　　pull you from your interminable grave.

You remember the dancing, the whirling, the unbounded joy
　　and expansive celebration that greeted you each morning.
You remember the women, their drums and chants rising to
　　mingle with honey scented air, timbrel and harp inter-
　　twining with the winds, long after the song of women
　　receded down the hill.

You blessed their children and their loves with your constant
　　presence.
Your fashioned body pressed into the nurturing earth, meeting
　　Yourself— forever caressed by the winds, connecting to the
　　magma deep within. Fire currents running deep, shifting,
　　changing shapes...

A volcano thousands of miles away exploding...
New visitors coming to the land, weapons held high, eyes
    sharp, pushing your body down to the soil.

The women no longer come.
Lonely voices whisper on the hillside circling endlessly
    through leaves and grasses, branches and trees finding no
    speaker nor listener.
Goddess, your body is laid down to sleep under the grains of
    time.
Covered more each year, only the insects of the soil visit you
    now.

Slanting tendrils of fire flood the dawnlit sky
Hands reaching down to lift you to light from your earthen
    grave,
Goddess what a story you have to tell.

Andrea Epel Lieberstein
Novato, California

Mother Nature's Desire

do you remember when we loved each other so deeply
that there was no separation between us?

we lived together in harmony, sweet harmony
and not just us
everyone lived in the same sweet harmony

one living entity all over this Mother Earth
under this Father Sun
we were all one
I loved you so then

when you used to listen to everything
when you spoke with the wind, the ocean, the rocks, the fire
and all of the other creatures that lived around you
when they spoke to you and you listened
yes, those were the good days

ah...such a sweet time
I miss it and I still long for it
those times before you became so clever
those times before you became so dirty
those times before the great betrayal

I still spend a great deal of time wondering
how it all went so wrong
what was the specific thing that turned you
into something so dangerous
into something so ugly
into something so selfish?

it's not like you didn't all have instructions
on how to be

The Original Instructions weren't complicated:
simply live in balance
respect everything around you
take only what you need
maintain connection to every thing
be harmonious

that was when you still remembered you were
part of something much greater than your self
when you sang to the stars and they sang back
it was such a joyous time
we were all so fulfilled
there could be no greater love
than the one I had for you
when you sang it filled me with joy

when you prayed it filled me with love
when you danced upon the belly of
our Mother, She knew your gratitude
when you charted Father Sun's movements
He knew you were paying attention
and He rejoiced in your knowledge

and now look at what you have done
you have become separate
what can possibly be worse than that?

and in your separateness you have
forgotten almost everything
you have poisoned your home
you have polluted everything you have touched
you have had no regard for all of your relations
you have killed without thought without prayer
you have regressed in to barbarity
you have become something unrecognizable
to all of those around you

and you wonder why I am upset
even angry
you wonder
why Mother Earth shakes

why Father Sun burns
why the Ocean wells up
why the Fire rages
why the Wind races

We are angry with you

We could wipe you out in one moment
if We so choose
but We still have hope for you
to come back to Us
to be one with Us
to live with the Original Instructions

step in to the circle
that you walked away from
it is time to choose
not much time left
do it now.

Pennie Opal Plant, 2008
Albany, California

It Is My Heart Who Reminds Me

That I shall weep over the grave of my desires
That I shall mourn over my failures
My long lost hope, mi copalera ardiendo and my ideas about
    Love
Love? is a little frozen man spinning on the palm of my right
    hand,
And I am the fool blowing kisses in the air.

It is my heart who reminds me
That I must weep over the loss of my illusion
That I shall mourn over my pride, my resistance turned poison
Of the blood stream like liquor, like shame
The piercing pain of violent raids
The broken will, the heavy load...

It is my heart who reminds me that I've been lost
On this river of oblivion, my face swollen with lies
My blood at war with itself; el Indigena Vs. el alienigena
Eternally killing and dying in the theaters of my flesh.

It is my heart who reminds me that I will cry
Blinded and bound by the laws of the empire,
By the gods of fear
FEAR

Is a broken feather on the palm of my left hand
And I? am the same fool...

But the crows are laughing you see and great winds are finally
    here
It has been written in stone that we got to remember the song
Totlazotlanazin Anuahuak cantame la cancion del jaguar
Corazon del monte, Tezkatlipoka
I am calling you back with all my essence
Calling you back with all my Soul
Calling you back from the cathedrals of genocide
Back from the realm of the white man
Back from the grid, the collapse of the dollar
From the federal reserve, from the memory of rape
Way back
Back with all my Soul,
Back, back, my jaguar is back!

And it is my heart who remembers that before I was called
    Woman
My name was keeper of wisdom, my name was sister, mother,
    precious child,
She who listens, owner of the fire of the house,
She who investigates deep down under the secrets of the
    cosmic mind,

The music of the inner god, the scent of precipitation-
   thunderous rapture of knowing, act of illumination.
 It is my heart who remembers a mis abuelas cantando
Sitting around the fire making food for hard times,
Food made with palabras de trueno, seeds to keep inside until
   the day comes,
Bitter roots for protection and the careful instruction
To hold hands
Open the eye on your chest
Stay strong
Be together for the first rays of dawn.

mi copalera ardiendo - Ardent Copal burner
el Indigena Vs. el alienígena - the Indigenous in me versus the
alien
Totlazotlanazin Anuahuak cantame la cancion del jaguar -
Beloved and respectable Mother Earth sing for me the song of
the Jaguar *Corazon del monte* - Heart of the Mountains
Tezkatlipoka - Internal Knowing
a mis abuelas cantando - my Grandmothers singing
palabras de trueno - words of thunder

Silvia Parra
Mission District, San Francisco

Footsteps
An Irish conachlann

I follow the footsteps of my foremothers Foremothers who gave birth to me Me, a priestess of the Goddess Goddess we draw down to us Us, the People of the Earth Earth that supports us all All life, even you and I I follow the footsteps of my foremothers.

Elizabeth Barrette
Charleston, Illinois

Invitation to Bridgit

We welcome you, Bridgit, on Imbolc Eve,
We ask for your blessing, new life to receive.
O Mother of poetry, teach us your art,
That your inspiration may enter each heart.

Oh, Mistress of Magic, who stands by the fire
And shapes the bright metal to form your desire.
Oh, Mother of Smithcraft, teach us your art.
That the power of change may enter each heart.

You kindle spring time to quicken the earth,
From your green mantle the old has new birth.
Oh, Mother of healing, please teach us your art
That the fire of renewal may kindle each heart.

Kate Wolf-Pizor
Mountain View, California

Grandmother Spider

Years ago I happened to be sitting near a spider web stretched between two dry branches. By shifting my point of view, I could see the entire landscape through a shimmering, intricate, transparent pattern. I never forgot my desert epiphany, and in 2004 I choreographed ritual performances based on the Native American legend of the Spider Woman. In 2007 I received an Alden Dow Fellowship which allowed me to weave several community art projects with Her grace.

Grandmother Spider is ubiquitous throughout the Americas. There is a legend that She will return at the end of this era (which, according to the Hopi calendar, is now.) Perhaps, the World Wide Web is her latest appearance.

The Navajo revere her for teaching them how to weave, and to this day, when a Navajo girl is born a bit of spider web is rubbed into the palms of her hands so she will "become a good weaver." May we all rub a bit of spider web into our hands now.

Spiderwoman Speaks

Listen, I'll tell you something.
Because you came here,
Listening to the wind.
Because you came here with your hands empty.

You don't know my name. It doesn't matter.
I've had a lot of names.
It doesn't matter what you call me.

Call me Tse-Che-Nako, call me Spider Woman.
Bring your offerings if you wish.
I'll give them to the Bird People, to the Mouse People

Listen, I'll tell you something.
Your spirit has become woven into bad things.
It' s time to weave a new story now.

Walk out into the desert and
sit beneath a cholla. Notice the shapes of things,
A hawk hunting against the sky. The shape of the sky,
Blue Mountain in the distance, the shapes of shadows,
The shape of your own shadows.

Take a deep breath,
A breath of all the stories that live here.
Stories like threads woven into the land.
Stories that wrap themselves
around old bones and pottery shards,
Stories running on four legs, and stories
written in the rocks about Snake and Raven,
The Yellow Women,
and the hearts of sleeping mountains.

And cracks in the land
like a spider web, full of light.

Once, you could see the Web
as plain as day. Song lines, leylines,
threads, connections, the pattern.
Each shining thread,
each shining, light woven thread.

You say you can't see it.
Well, take a look around!
You don't need to climb a mountain
to get the big picture!

All of its snaking rivers
and twining roots
Are inside of you!
All those threads
come right out of your hands
And out of your hearts
All those threads just go on forever

Into the Earth,
and into each other,
into all your stories,
into everyone you'll ever know,
into all those who came before you,
and all those who will come after you.

Lauren Raine
International Nomad

Psalm 86/Sophia Responsorial

Prayer, adapted, arr. Evelie Delfino Sáles Posch

© February 26th, 2009

© *Evelie Delfino Sáles Posch*
El Cerrito, California

The Blessing

I stand on my world's edge, breathing rich sea air,
Embracing early morning's chill...listening...
Luminous full moon, bright in western sky
Ocean singing rhythmic hushabyes
Sparkling liquid curls...phosphorescent quicksilver hums
Electric undulating depths whisper, "Be still...magic's in
    the air."

Morning's sun sends orange beacons into night's sky
Highlighting floating scoops of billowy orange sherbet,
Dawn melts night and drips its illumination upon waters
Turning midnight blue into golden orange
Flaunting unlikely nocturnal edges against dawn
Spreading surprised color splashes upon land and water.

A shaft...prismed color arcs out from watery base
Gathering intensity and hue, it reaches toward shore
Hillsides sleepy with dew respond
Awakening their column of colors, arching toward sea.
A perfect rainbow...vibrant...vital...bridging water and land.

A second shaft arises, echoing the first...could it be true?
Could nature's blessing be more generous...more abundant?

The tease of second promise would suffice for unbelieving
    eyes,
Yet rainbows shine their full spectrum twice.
Incredulous awe bows to wonder, every morsel, every image
    absorbed.

Cliff's edge follows smooth shoreline curve
South into Monterey ... north into Santa Cruz
I stand alone on the edge of all possible worlds.
At surf's edge directly below my cliffside view
One lone man unknowingly shares my solitude.
I stand in this moment with all of life honoring itself.

Una Nakamura, 1997
San Francisco Bay Area

Madonna Virgo Dolorosa

Queen of love and pain and sadness.
Long-suffering Lady of Perpetual Sorrows,
Purified by Her tears.
Who pursues the path of selfless service,
Care-filled healing and heartfelt passion
To heights and depths and breadths unfathomed.
Who practices faith and patience, infinite persistence.
Who plunges directly through the darkness,
Through the swamps and sweats and sucking shallows,
Through twisted tunnels and around blind bends,
Through delusion, through denial, through to destined ends.

Donna Henes
Brooklyn, New York

Charge of the Queen

I am woman of the sky.
I am woman of the grave.
I am mirror of the moon.
I am reflection of the day.

I am song of the wind.
I am river of the rain.
I am pulse of the stars.
I am churn of the deep.

I am child of the daughter.
I am sister of all sisters.
I am woman of the woman.
I am mother of myself.

I am defender of the beauty.
I am midwife of the change.
I am creator of the vision.
I am lover of it all.

Donna Henes
Brooklyn, New York

To The Lady With Parsley Hair

Reverence to you, Green Lady
Made of lettuce and zucchini
With radishes strategically placed
And berry eyes...

You might have been funny or cute—
But when the drumming started
You turned somehow elemental,
Like a clay poppet smeared with blood,
Creating the wellspring of power
That makes primate nostrils flare.

But your power was life force
Humming and pushing up
From dark, hidden places into light;
No dainty doings here, but power to
Move anything we might dare
To put in your way.

Even vegetable Ladies, smiling,
Show teeth.

Beth Marshall
St. Petersburg, Florida

Invocation to Elah

Elah great mother self
Goddess of vision
One who crowns women with profound gifts of vision.
One who forms women in her own image to see herself
    consciously,
and not just in the shadow of her dreams.
Elah, great mother earth who creates from earth
One who shares intimate secrets of death and rebirth in the
    whispers of women
and within the wisdom of serpents and dark birds.
Elah, tree women, high priestess of the forest,
One who exists within many worlds at once.
Your eyes and words move slowly, carefully,
as you realize that all that is said
affects time and space irrevocably.
Goddess mother self,
the me innana gains
the selfhood of both eternal divinity and earthly mortality.
The blessing, the wrestling, the irony.
Elah
The space between spirit and form
The courage of existence,
The strength to endure,

to carry on amidst suffering and forgetfulness.

The shedding of old forms so that life can begin again.

Elah, great mother force that calls me to know the presence of the one

through the womb and the belly.

Elah, blessed force of gravity that returns me to my roots in eternity.

jme* ismyn
Oakland, California

Blessings of Yemaya

I have come to you Mother of waves and foam,
Diosa del Mar, Goddess of blue waters
Know that I can feel you in the salt water in my veins
Your beautiful loving heart is in my heart
And your fierceness sometimes takes me
To where I cannot see.

I have come to you Mother of ocean womb,
Mama Wata, Star of the Sea
Know that I can taste you in the salt water of my tears
Your ancient wisdom flows through my mind
And your female power takes me
To where I can be healed.

I have come to you Mother of dreams and secrets,
Olodumare, Owner of the Rainbow
Know that I can hear you as a voice in my ears
Your dark luscious body appears in my dreams
And the dance of your joy takes me
To where I can rejoice.

Tina Proctor
Denver, Colorado

Invocation

I am flowing beauty, I am
The watery realm of passion electrifying the blood I am
The softness of skins touching,
An opening rose kissed
By dew I am the freshness of morning, the
Depth of breath drawn into open lungs I am
The loving gaze of eyes engulfed
In beauty I am

The fragrant spice in nectars I am
Fields of bloom, the buzz
Of bees eager for sweetness,
The flight of birds in the sun I am
Smooth motion of dolphins, the playfulness of seals,
The warmth of flesh alive I am

The thirst and the drink and the quench I am

DeAnna L'am, © 1995
Santa Rosa, California

White Tārā Meditation

Each day I pray for my loved ones, those whom I know to be ill, and those who have requested that I pray for them. I begin by invoking White Tārā, the goddess of long life, wealth, good health, and success. I chant her mantra at least seven times: OM TARE TUTARE TURE MAMA AYUH PUNYA JNANA PUSHTIM KURU SVAHA. As translated by Stephan Beyer in his Cult of Tārā: Magic and Ritual in Tibet, this means "[Mother Tārā] increase my life, merit, and knowledge!" (210). I follow this by chanting the mantra of Green Tārā 108 times: OM TARE TUTARE TURE SOHA! The frequent recitation of this mantra is said to bring about the elimination of fear and sickness, and grant success. The OM connotes "the goal of the path." TARE is Tārā: "She who liberates us from suffering." TUTARE means: "She who eliminates all fears." TURE is "she who grants all successes." SOHA reminds us to rejoice as the mantra takes "root in our hearts" ("Praises to Tārā" 1). I wear a mala, a link of 108 prayer beads, so that I can chant one round to Green Tārā at least three times daily.

There are twenty-one praises to Aryā, or Noble, Tārā in all her twenty-one forms, or manifestations. I honor her by reciting these three times each day, ideally at morning, noon, and night, but sometimes all at once. I then conclude with a prayer of veneration.

Because I believe we are all interconnected or interrelated in this web of life, my happiness, future as well as ultimate happiness, relies upon the happiness of all other sentient beings. For this reason, I try to be a better human being. True happiness lies within our interactions with one another. I do this by confessing my downfalls to my guru, or teacher, Tārā and the 35 Confession Buddhas. I meditate on the visualization of White Tārā, recite mantras, do prostrations, and pray to do better in all my interactions with my fellow beings.

White Tārā Meditation

The following meditation is a sort of pastiche. It is reminiscent of the meditations of other Tibetan Buddhist deities; however, it contains some original descriptions of White Tārā's appearance to aid in her visualization.

Before we begin the visualization, we take a moment to set the intention or motivation for meditating on White Tārā. She is known for granting long life, wealth, and wisdom to all who request it of her. We first ask for these wonderful qualities for ourselves, our loved ones, and our teachers such as His Holiness the 14th Dalai Lama, Tenzin Gyatso.

At the crown of our head, we visualize White Tārā. She is a beautiful woman in the prime of life with a full figure. She is called white because of the luminous light that emanates from every pore of her body. She embodies all the great wisdom of glorious beings like the Buddhas and Bodhisattvas. She is seated in the full lotus posture. Her right hand is on her right knee in the gesture of granting her supreme realization. In her left hand she holds the stem of the Utpala flower, a large blue lotus. She has seven eyes: one on each hand and foot, and a third between the normal eyes on her face. These eyes symbolize the watchfulness of her compassionate mind. Her whole body is the nature of radiant light.

The syllable TĀM reaches out from her heart. Its light rays shine forth and seize all the life force that has been scattered, stolen, or confiscated. This dissolves into the TĀM, into the light. Then again these light rays return emitting from the TĀM to bestow the power and blessings of all the Buddhas and Bodhisattvas. This, too, dissolves into TĀM. The four elements: earth, water, fire, and air; and the element of space absorb into TĀM and emit a rainbow of light and sweet flowing nectar like honey.

All of this beautiful light and nectar flow from this seed syllable TĀM into the body through the crown. Our entire body is filled with this light and nectar that eliminates everything negative: any obstructions, all disease, any harm from negative intentions, and the danger of untimely death.

All these negative things leave our body in the form of dirty liquid, and our body becomes pure and clear like crystal. Our mind becomes clear and blissful. Think and truly believe:

at this moment I am free of everything negative. Now we recite her mantra: OM TARE TUTARE TURE MAMA AYUH PUNYA JNANA PUSHTIM KURU SVAHA!

Karen Nelson Villanueva
San Francisco, California

My Secret Story

Deep in your warm waters
Stardust impregnated your womb
and I was born ...
Bonded to you then
Remembering you now
Oh joyful Mothers Day!

I knew you as creatrix, moon, sun and stars
and sat in your tree of wisdom among
the snakes and birds -
I smelled the air
and became strong, conscious and loved...

I was almost destroyed when you were scarped
and I was left helpless at the soul of violence
Oh, unhappy knowledge... I have walked such
a dry road — but I have found you...
and we wept; as did Persephone and Demeter.

May your winged spirit soar free and your
story be told and peace be in your body
Before we are all stardust...

Amen with joy, oh found Mother.

Jayne DeMente, 2009
Los Angeles, California

Queen

I stand alone and not
surrounded by my sisters, friends, mothers
gone before and those still present here
in an ancient stream passed on passed through.
I hold my ground, stake my claim
as a woman found, bound by none but Love.
With open hands I warm myself at my own heart fire.
Keeper of the Hearth, I fan the flame,
   tell the Stories,
       rock the babies,
          teach what's true.

I grant myself immunity from all heartless,
soul-less, mindless methods and machinations
of those who don't know better.
I own my blood wisdom tucked safely
in my ovaries and womb, stronger than any lie.
Hands on my belly, I bless its fruit — four babies grown!
Thank you! Yes, thank you,
for your bloody birth gifts and monthly blood flow.
I release my seeds now to plant something new
and unexpected, birthed from my Love alone.

Oh, yes! Ain't I a Woman* now?
I've been to the dark,
faced my shadows, wept, bled, and died,
returning to count myself among the blessed born.

I raise my heart in strong surrender to the old new path
I choose to take.
I am the Grand Mother and I call on the Great Mothers of all—
Kali-Ma, Isis, Inanna, Mother Mary, Yemaya, Mary Magdalene,
Kuan Yin, Tara, Prajnaparamita, Vajravarahi, and White Buddha Dakini to assist me as I open my heart back up to myself
and to the world.

Blessed Be!

Pauline E. Reif
San Francisco Bay Area

---

*From speech presented by Sojourner Truth at women's rights convention
in Akron, Ohio, 1851.

When life is presenting a great deal of change

O Oya, O mama

I come to you mama in this moment of change and changes
    in my life
I ask you to guide me through them.

O Oya, O mama,

I look to you mama, to provide me with an understanding,
    to lift my confusion, to help me to take a risk into the
    unknowing with the knowledge that my landing will be
    safely protected by you.

O Oya, O mama,

Guide me Oya, as a light into the unforeseen let the breeze
    carry your words in the wind for me to hear and follow.
Keep me from whirling out of control, dizzy with confusion not
    knowing what to do.

O Oya, O mama

Hold me mama as I flow with life's changes embracing them as
    you embrace me.

Rashidah Tutashinda, 2009
Oakland, California

Listen to the call

There is a primordial scream
rising from deep within woman bellies* . . .
can you hear it?
It reverberates through the land in many forms
seen and unseen,
heard and unspoken . . . .
It is the deep ache of the loss of a mother—known, but
forgotten.

She is calling us – the Divine Mother.
She calls us from within ourselves;
beckoning us back to our true nature,
the order of the Divine Woman.
There is no one religion, or practice, that we need to embrace...
the path is a way of being.

Listen to the call.
Bring it forth, in your own precious way.
Honor that which is "woman" . . .
and see the great change that it brings to the world.

Donna DeNomme, 2005
Golden, Colorado

---

*Author's Note: "woman bellies" is not a typo, but intentional wording.

The Practical Priestess

I have been summoned
And I will come
Shaking my rattle, beating
My drum
Laden with pomegranates
And honey
And lest I forget,
The much needed money
And in great elation
How happy I'll be
To find an occasion
To celebrate ME!!!

Kaye Schuman, 2007
New Jersey

U'vachein, And Then

U'vachein, u'vachein, and then and then
When wholeness and peace are restored
U'vachein, u'vachein, and then and then
Remembering what all life is for

In awe and afraid, taking stock of our days
Healed by forgiveness and love
We pray a time will come as we return to the One
That we can become truly one

U'vachein, u'vachein, and then and then
When wholeness and peace are restored
U'vachein, u'vachein, and then and then
Remembering what all life is for

When reverence for life is the prayer that unites
All people as one family
Remembering our light, a spark of the divine in ourselves
and in all living beings

(Bridge)

Then, and then, just the sound of it
Gives wings to hope, lays fear to rest
To feel the open wings of possibility
Then and then, imagine.....

When I can glimpse or locate a piece of the divine in me, it is a sense of Divine Love whose quality is the Mother of All Life. In singing in the sacred, I direct my energy toward her. Our gratitude is Her nourishment. I sing in her arrival, a Holy Guest, the Shechinah who is always waiting for us to come home.

The Sacred Feminine for me is the Shechinah—the one who dwells in harmonious exchanges and places of kindness and beauty—this is the place where all transformation is possible. It is an open and vulnerable energy where sensitivity IS strength and where our heart's passion, wisdom and direction is affirmed.

She writes through me, of course. When my longing is the greatest, her angels answer me in song.

Alisa Fineman
Pacific Grove, California

Holy Mary, Mother God

Hail, Mary, full of grace. We are one with thee.
Blessed art thou among all living.
And blessed are the creative fruits of thy Virginity,
springing forth in new images and new life.

Holy Mary, Mother God,
From your breasts flow fountains of living water.
From your maternal deep,
we are born again unto self-love and self-celebration.

Patricia Lynn Reilly
Western Michigan

Kali 1

Oh Kali ma mother of fearsome night

I search for you on shelves
and find
— nothing

words

Your story is not in the letters
but in the dance of letters
trampling the page

Alphabets are not enough
and so I must dance your dance
to know you

in a parking lot

in the woods

under a watchfulness
a caring a surprise a knowing a blessing

I will write you with my body
educate with orgasms
learn from the text I write
— myself

Elka Eastly Vera
San Francisco, California

Kali

Kali Ma, blessed mother of black blood,
My anger brings you with its surging flood.
Eager for burning flesh, your tongue hangs low,
The light from your third eye blinds those below.
Your shining blade held aloft sings its dirge—
A necklace of skulls chants the sinister urge
And hangs round your neck with an aching weight:
Who can face the raw carnage of fury's fate?
Kali Ma! Join the circle, heed my call!
Help me, when I'm angry, to still stand tall,
To feel my power, my sorrow, my wrath,
To know that terror is part of my path.
Mother of darkness, of blood deeds, and pain,
Purge my heart of its bitterness once again.

K. A. Laity
Watervliet, New York

If birth were a temple

If birth were a temple,
my body is religion, and this small form
twisting out of me,

is

prayer

my cries
reach birth's vaulted
ceilings,

arching like my back over holy
waters,
crystal clear salt of amniotic

my womb—a blessing bowl
releases
her treasure.

Nané Ariadne Jordan
Vancouver, British Columbia

Evangelio Segun Magdalena -
The Gospel of Mary Magdalene

En aquellos tiempos existia una mujer
de nombre Maria Magdalena
Le nombraban el discipulo mas amado.
Mujer de misterios, sacerdotisa ponderosa

Por haber manchado tu nombre
La iglesia te implora perdón.

Madgalena, apostol de apostoles
Renunciaste a todo por estar con el amado
Le serviste al maestro de espejo
Para crecer hacia la integración, en relación

Madgalena nos robaron tu historia
Nos hicieron creer que eras una prostituta
Lo mas amado por el Cristo lo mancharon de fango

Por intentar destruir tu evangelio
La iglesia te implora perdón.

Madalena fuiste tu la elegida
A la hora de la resurección

Por dos mil años de mentiras
La iglesia te implora perdón.

Maria Madalena... ruega por ellos
Maria Madalena... despiertalos
Maria Madalena... ten piedad de ellos
Maria Madalena... perdónalos

In the beginning, there was a woman
named Mary Magdalene
she was called the most beloved disciple
a woman of mysteries, powerful priestess.

Because we stained your name
The church implores your forgiveness.

Magdalene, apostle of the apostles
You who renounced all comfort to be with the Beloved
You who acted as his mirror
To help him achieve integration through a loving relationship.

Magdalene they stole your story
They made us believe your were a prostitute
The most beloved by the Christ was covered with mud

For trying to destroy your gospel
The church implores your forgiveness.

Magdalene, you were the chosen
At the time of the resurrection

For two thousand years of lies
The church implores forgiveness.

Mary Magdalene... beg for them
Mary Magdalene... help them to wake up
Mary Magdalene... have mercy for them
Mary Magdalene... forgive them

Aurora Medina
San Francisco Bay Area

My Explanation

Pick up a stone.
Hold it in your hand.
Feel the vibration?
Pick up a leaf.
Trace the vines.
Feel the life?
Climb a tree.
Trust the sturdy branches.
Feel the stability?
Go out side right before a storm.
Hear the thunder, watch the lightening.
Feel the energy building?
Lie down in a field on a cool day when the sun is shining.
Feel it surround you with warmth and safety?
Stand up and turn around in cirlces.
Feel the wind rush through your hair.
Feel the spirit?
Go out to that same field at night when the moon is full.
Let the moon light guide your way.
Feel the magic?
As you look up to the sky
and count the stars
know that they hold no prejudice, no hate, and no judgment.

Know that you have a home in the universe (which means
   one song)
as long as you know that you are a part of all that
   surrounds you
and all that surrounds you is a part of you.
The vibration you felt in the rock,
the life in the leaf,
the stability of the tree,
the energy of the storm,
the warmth of the sun,
the spirit in the wind,
the magic of the moon,
and the unconditional love of the stars,
know those are your gods and goddesses,
and the earth is your bible.
Everything possesses a spark of divinity, including you.
You need to look no further than the world around you,
or your own mirror
to find God(dess) and know where you belong.
That is my religion.

Diana "Sollitaire" H.
North Texas

She Dances The World Forth

She dances the world forth
from black and blue
rolled out and pressed down.
She circles and dives
The world comes forth.

Wind spilling upon caves hidden under the sea.

She dances the world forth
breathing through snakes and trees
and shapes unformed.
Time spreads out upon her body
whirling like silken threads
upon the spider's web.
She dances the world forth.

I went away. I forgot you.
My tongue tastes the saltiness of your return.

She dances the world forth
between dusk and fog.

The sound of her appearance
reverberates within my sleeping spine
tickles my tailbone
teases me inside out
calls me forth.

The triangle unfolds rich power
as the never before knocks at my door.

She dances the world forth
in resplendent darkness.
Camelia blossoms float on my belly.
A bowl of liquid fire rests within my throat.

She dances the world forth.

Louise Pare, 1996
Ashland, Oregon

A prayer to be spoken for those
who have lost someone through death

I come to you in this moment of sorrow and grief standing
   fearless in the face of death/birth.
I come to you releasing my hold, embracing my love, and with
   an understanding of continuation.
I come to you in this moment of deep sadness Mama, pouring
   libation with my tears, offering my grief for memories of
   joy.
I come asking you to lift the weight of this sorrow from my
   heart, to release the pain, to heal the numbness, to silence
   my inner screams.
I come to you asking for help in accepting this death, as it
   births into a new reality and to celebrate it.

Rashidah Tutashinda, 2009
Oakland, California

Praises to Ishtar

Ishtar za-mi* Hallelu-hi

אשתר זמי הללוהי

Berucha at, Elah D'vash,

ברכה את אלה דבש

In lips you are sweet, all life is in your mouth

Hallelu Isha S'tar, Elat nora'ah ba'elot

praise woman of mystery, most awesome of the goddesses

הללו אשה סתר אלת ירת קבוד

Kavdu malkat nashim, kabirah mikol elot

revere the queen of women, greatest of goddesses

קבדו מלכת נשים כבירה מכל אלות

You are laden with vitality

Life drips from your mouth

Diburim d'vash, min d'viriech korei kol haneshama

mouth (words) of honey, from your holy of holies

all beings cry out

דבורים דבש מן דביריך קרה כל הנשמה

Your lips are sweet, for all life is born through them

All life is in your mouth, and it is sweet

Toledot chai tiftafu m'pich

---

*Sumerian: Praise Ishtar

all life drips from your mouth

תולדת חי תפתפו מפך

Honey drops onto my lips, tzufit tiftuf
and I sing Your praises

D'vora K'lilah, 2007*
San Francisco, California

---

*Editor's note: From the ancient Babylonian prayer, translated by D'vora
from English to Hebrew

A Celebration of Her, and of Life
(A reinterpretation of the traditional Jewish Kaddish memorial prayer)

Blessed Be G'd, Shekhinah
In this world of Her creation
May Her will be fulfilled
And her vision and wisdom be revealed
So that our own purpose may become ever clearer
In the days of our lifetime
Speedily and soon
And let us say Amen.

May Her great name be blessed forever
May the name and qualities of the Sacred Feminine
be embodied in us all
May they be praised and honored,
Remembered and celebrated
Observed and protected, at our very core
and in all our words and acts.

Blessed be She
Beyond all blessings and hymns,
Praises and petitions
That we may utter in this world

To this we say Aṣẹ and Amen.

May peace and abundance,
a sense of direction and courage
fill us,
surround us
and keep us.

May your heart give us life
And let us say Blessed Be.
May She Who creates
The harmony of the universe

Who enriches our sight
And protects our being
Nourishes our spirit
And gives us hope,
Create peace for us and all who dwell in the world.
And let us say
Aṣẹ and Amen.

*D'vorah J. Grenn, 2007**
Napa, California

---

*Originally written for the Mishkan Shekhinah temple prayerbook.

About These Amazing Women

Chandra Alexandre, Ph.D., D.Min., MBA is Rashani (Priestess) and Executive Director of SHARANYA, a federally-recognized devi mandir (goddess temple) dedicated to an embodied and engaged spirituality that facilitates the life-affirming transformation of individuals, communities and our world. SHARANYA's is a (R)evolutionary Western Shakta Tantra. Visit us at: www.SHARANYA.org or at our online mystery school, Kali Vidya, at www.kalividya.org. Jai Maa!

Laura Amazzone, M.A. is a writer, jewelry designer, teacher, priestess and yogini. Laura is presently completing a book on the Goddess Durga and Her annual fall festival that will be published by Hamilton Books, an imprint of University Press, in 2010. She has traveled extensively throughout South and Southeast Asia doing on-site research to investigate the relationship between women's spiritual and sexual empowerment and the Goddess Durga in her various forms. Laura currently lives in Venice, California with her cat Gypsy and teaches classes on the Shakta Tantra tradition and Goddesses in Santa Monica and at Loyola Marymount University. Laura has been creating sacred adornment for over 20 years. Her line of amuletic goddess necklaces can be found at http://www.amazzonejewelry.com.

Uzuri Amini is a priestess of Oshun, the Yoruba goddess of love, healing and art. The Oshun Society in Oshogbo, Nigeria, initiated her in the spring of 1989. A 21st century Renaissance woman, Uzuri is a writer, artist and ceremonialist. As a spiritual counselor, she developed and facilitates various workshops from Ancestor Reverence to helping Survivors of Childhood Sexual Abuse get a chance to release and do healing work. Uzuri is published in *The Goddess Celebrates, Earthwalking Skydancers* and *A Waist is a Terrible Thing to Mind.* She is also a faculty member of the School of Ancient Mysteries/Sacred Arts Center in Oakland, California.

Michele Arista has her M.A. in Women's Spirituality from New College of California. Michele Arista is a Health Physicist and a Ph.D. candidate at the California Institute of Integral Studies, specializing in ecofeminism and feminist philosophy. Arista is a published poet and sacred artist and the owner of the Dance International Studio for belly dance in Manchester, NH. Her art can be seen in OCRE Journal of Women's Spirituality, fall 2007. She seeks to create images, poetry and dance shapes which connect women with the Divine Feminine and the Sacred Earth.

Mariam Baker is dedicated to embodied spirituality as a tool for personal and planetary healing and peace. Mariam is known as a spiritual midwife and energy weaver. She is a senior teacher (Atesh Baz) and center leader of the Mevlevi Order of America , facilitating classes and performance of the work of Mevlana Jelaluddin Rumi, including the TURN of the whirling dervish.

Initiate in the Inayati Chistia lineage of Sufism through Hazrat Inayat Khan and Murshid Samuel Lewis, she was student of the late Moineddin Jablonski. She facilitates group and individual Sufi Soulwork, a way toward spiritual and psychological integration. Mariam is an active member and senior teacher (Murshid) of Sufi Ruhaniat International and a leader in the Dances of Universal Peace since 1974.

Mariam has served as a guide and ritualist in women's and religious studies, presenting lectures, retreats and workshops in the US, Canada, Europe, Australia, South America, and Africa. She is the former director of Theater of Healing and author of Woman as Divine, Tales of the Goddess, a dance drama illuminating the divine feminine.

Elizabeth Barrette has been involved with the Pagan community for more than twenty-one years, including study of comparative religions and interfaith work. She served as Managing Editor of PanGaia for 8 years and Dean of Studies at the Grey School of Wizardry for 4 years. Her book Composing Magic explains how to write spells, rituals, and other Pagan material. She lives in central Illinois and enjoys herbal landscaping and gardening for wildlife. She has done much networking with Pagans in her area, including coffeehouse meetings and open sabbats. Her other writing fields include speculative fiction and gender studies. Visit her blogs "The Wordsmith's Forge" (http://ysabetwordsmith.livejournal.com); "Gaiatribe: Ideas for a Thinking Planet" (http://gaiatribe.geekuniversalis.com.)

Valgerður H. Bjarnadóttir has her M.A. in Women's Spirituality and BA in Integral Studies from CIIS, with a degree in Social Work from Bærum, Norway as well. She has worked with women's issues for three decades in many areas of life. She is the founder & freyja of

Auður Valgerðar, and its main project Vanadís – our roots, dreams and power (www.vanadis.is), where she teaches, gives counseling and consultations for individuals and groups, writes, conducts research and arranges rituals, events, work-shops, seminars and conferences for the Goddess and her messengers. Valgerður is a lover of stories, myths and adventure, and in her workshops, counseling and writing she entwines self-imaging, myths, folktales and sagas, dreams, rituals, shamanic worldview, dreaming and interaction with Nature.

Valgerður has had a profound love for the Goddess in her many guises as long as she can remember. In her MA she looked for the traces of Goddess culture and shamanic endeavours in the Icelandic Sagas and poems. Currently she is writing a book on women's self-esteem and another on Inanna and Enheduanna, where she translates the poems to Icelandic. Valgerður lives in Northern Iceland.

Sarah Blogg has an M.A. in Women's Spirituality from New College of California, San Francisco. Dancer, poet, ritualist, Sarah migrated to Australia after graduating, where she teaches and celebrates life.

Anne Bluethenthal, MFA is Founder and Artistic Director of ABD Productions, a multi-ethnic and multi-cultural modern dance company, committed to activism in the arts. A woman centered, collaborative dance ensemble, ABD is dedicated to creating a language of movement that breaks the ordinary paradigm of western dance and to presenting choreographies that face difficult issues with eloquence and passion. Through her choreography and community collaborations, Bluethenthal has presented work on subjects such as Palestine-Israel, globalization, the environment, genocide, and the gift economy. ABD received the SF Chronicle's Best of 2001 and the SF Bay Guardian's Goldie Award for Achievement in Dance.

Bluethenthal founded and produced the San Francisco Lesbian and Gay Dance Festival as well as the Dancing the Mystery series, a festival of dance, music and poetry celebrating women's spiritual traditions. Certified by the American and London Societies for Teachers of the Alexander Technique, Bluethenthal maintains a private teaching practice. She is on the faculties of the MA Women's Spirituality Program at Institute for Transpersonal Psychology and the Acting Program at Academy of Art University.

Carolyn Brandy, one of the foremothers of the Global Movement of Women Drummers, and founder of the non-profit Women Drummers International in 1998 is a composer, performer, and educator, and has worked in the Bay Area for many years. She was the founder of Sistah Boom, and was also a founding member of the all women jazz quintet Alive! which toured nationally for ten years, and produced three albums, released on a compilation CD, Always Alive! Carolyn released a self-produced CD of her own compositions in 1995, entitled Skin Talk.

Carolyn's most recent projects include the group OJALÁ, a vocal and percussion creative ensemble that mixes Cuban and American song forms. She is also the co-producer and founder of Born to Drum Women's Drum Camp, created in 2006 to inspire and empower women students and teachers of hand percussion. The camps have all been overwhelmingly successful, and offer a rare opportunity to study with "maestra" women drummers—from around the world.

Carolyn has been a drummer and student of Cuban folkloric music for over 40 years. A practitioner of the Yoruba-based Cuban religion, Regla de Ocha, also known as Santeria, since 1977, she was initiated as a priest of the religion in Havana, Cuba by Amelia Pedroso in 2000.

Carolyn has led five tours to the Island of Cuba to study Folkloric music and dance. She has organized workshops in Havana, Matanzas, Cienfuegos, Camaguey, Santiago De Cuba, Guantanamo, and Baracoa where the groups have studied with masters of Afro-Cuban drumming and dance. She has a degree in music from Holy Names University in Oakland. For more information about her activities, write to: cbrandydrum@sbcglobal.net or see http://www.borntodrum.org.

Christine Brooks, Ph.D., is an assistant professor at the Institute of Transpersonal Psychology. Areas of scholarship include intentional childlessness as a life path; archetypes and gender; transformational education, and feminist and queer spiritualities. She is currently working on a book, *Being True to Myself: The Life Path of Intentional Childlessness,* and has just launched an online survey on Third Wave Feminism and Spirituality. She can be contacted at cbrooks@itp.edu.

Christine's piece was written as she was conducting dissertation research on intentionally childless women. "During this time, my own experience of the goddess was not represented in the imagery of the Great Mother. I longed for an adult, fully-realized image of the divine feminine that was not tied in any way to mothering, but was also not relegated to maidenhood for life. "Christine wrote this piece to call in the other aspects of strong womanhood to support her in her journey toward self-realization "so that I would have the strength to tell the stories entrusted to me by other women who have chosen the path less travelled."

Sauda Burch was initiated for Oshun, the Orisa of the River, and the goddess of healing in1999. She has been a member of Ile Orunmila Oshun since 1992. As a priest she focuses on sacred song and on building and sustaining relationship with our Ancestors.

Sadhvi Vrnda Chaitanya is a Vedic scholar, a Monk, and the spiritual head of the Arsha Vijnana Mandiram, a center for the study of Vedanta and Sanskrit. She is also active in the interfaith movement for fostering mutual respect and harmony among religions. She travels, teaches, and writes about Vedanta and Vedic culture. Website address: www.arshavm.org.

Max Dashú is a researcher and teacher of women's cultural heritages. She founded the Suppressed Histories Archives in 1970 to research global women's history, archaeology, goddesses, shamans, and mother-right. She has archived over 15,000 slides and created

100 visual talks, which she has presented at universities, community centers, and conferences. See her new poster of ancient Female Icons from around the world at www.suppressedhistories.net, as well as articles, book excerpts, and clips from the Women's Power DVD. Max is also a founding mother of the Goddess resurgence, a Pagan elder, and a visionary artist. Her art has appeared in books, magazines, calendars and the Daughters of the Moon Tarot. Her fine prints, note-cards, and magnets can be seen at http://www.maxdashu.net.

Patti Davis has an M.A., in Philosophy & Religion/Women's Spirituality, CIIS, San Francisco, California. Multi-traditional ritualist, sacred artist & altar creatrix.

Cheryl Dawson has an M.A., Women's Spirituality; M. Div. candidate at Graduate Theological Union, Berkeley. Poet, writer and spiritual leader.

Jayne DeMente has a Masters in Women's Spirituality from the California Institute of Integral Studies. She is the founder/director of Women's Heritage Project, a ten-year-old endowment program granting scholarships to students and institutes of higher learning in the field of women's spirituality. She has written a textbook, "Feminine Reformation; a goddess meta-narrative", and co-hosts the radio talk show "Creatrix Media Live" at BlogTalkRadio.com. See www.womensheritageproject.ning.com for more information.

Donna DeNomme is a conscious energy teacher, self-actualization facilitator, licensed spiritual coach, and ceremonial leader. Donna has a degree in Human Development and Families Studies from Cornell University, an advanced certification in spiritual counseling, and many years training in alternative therapies, and indigenous healing practices. She is the founder and director of Inlightened Source Productions, assisting women since1987. www.inlightenedsource.com.

Donna is a national motivational speaker and is the author of an award-winning book, *Turtle Wisdom: Coming Home to Yourself*, now being published in several languages. She is also the co-author of a girls' inspirational book series, *Ophelia's Oracle*, sharing ancient divine feminine stories, as well as their relevance for young girls today. See her website for more information: www.opheliasoracle.com.

Suzanne De Veuve, artist and painter, grew up in Palo Alto, California and always wanted to be an artist. "Even though I was encouraged as a child to draw, paint and sculpt, my family thought painting was no way to make a living, so I didn't have any reason to think I could make a living from art. For years I just kept doing other things for work, trying to be responsible. But in my spare time, I would paint and draw." Suzanne worked as a nurse's aid, took classes to become a registered nurse and even considered becoming a marine biologist because of her love for nature and the ocean.

"In college, where art was presented as something strict and formal, I actually flunked out of an art class. We had to do things like make color charts with a hundred shades of gray from white to black. I could never do art with my left brain; I realized that way of learning art was not going to be my way. My way is just in doing it." Suzanne later attended the Academy of Arts in San Francisco and has been a painter for more than twenty years. A big part of her motivation to paint was wanting to bring out the ancient traditions and wisdom of women. "I've always felt very strongly that women need to integrate more of the ancient wisdom into our psyches to balance the high-tech developments of the past hundred years...As mothers and nur-turers, we have a lot to say and our voices help create a balance of power." See http://www.suzannedeveuve.com/.

Cosi Fabian was born on Malta, educated in England and the Far East, and has lived in San Francisco for much of her life. Called by Inanna, tutored by Ereshkigal and inspired by Lilith, at the age of 42 Cosi took on the experiment of living as an ancient Ishtaritu, a hierodule, a Sacred Prostitute. As mythologist, ritualist, teacher and contemporary courtesan, Cosi embodied and expressed the archetypal "Sacred Prostitute." Her essay "Holy Whore, a Woman's Gateway to Power" appeared in Whores and Other Feminists, pub-lished by Routledge. Cosi's groundbreaking research on ancient and new ways to look at women's sexuality has won her the respect and gratitude of women of all ages. She has been counseling for 20 years, teaching on and off for 14.

A published poet and popular storyteller, Cosi interweaves pre-patri-archal texts, modern psychology and her personal experience as a goddess-dedicated prostitute to banish shame, and re-choreograph the dance of women, men, sex and spirit. Her work has been influential in the development of the Women's Spirituality movement, and sex-positive feminism. She has appeared on network and international television and taught both privately and at San Francisco Bay Area universities and conferences. Living quietly in San Francisco, Cosi has retired from the front lines of women's spiritual sexuality and is currently writing her memoirs.

Iyanifa Fasina (Sheila Carr) is a Priest/ess of Ogun and Ifa, and continues the work of Ifa with workshops, consultations, divination, and traditional herbal medicine (iyanifa32@gmail.com.)

Alisa Fineman began learning guitar at age 11, and a year later was writing her first songs. Alisa's songs speak of love, of a sense of place and an appreciation for the earth's beauty and fragility, and of life's sometimes difficult choices.

She was voted "Best Folk Musician" four years running by the Monterey Bay's Coast Weekly and has toured extensively, appearing at festivals across the country. For the past fifteen years she has been increasingly called upon to contribute her talents as a cantorial soloist at celebratory events and at several synagogues in Northern California. She also is an active member of Ya Elah!, a spiritual and interfaith ensemble working to inspire unity through sacred text. She and her partner and fellow-musician Kimball Hurd recently released their new CD "Faith In our Love." For more information about her work, see www.alisafineman.com.

Dr. April Lea Go Forth, a ni yv wi'ya from Eastern Band of the Cherokee Nation, is a drumkeeper and singer. She is founding member of the women's drum "Thoz Womenz", a 2007 nominee of two Native American Music Awards. As an educator in her Native community she serves in diverse areas from health and education to parenting and cultural activities. Always, she brings in a woman's perspective on the healing power and guidance of the drum. In her teachings, April seeks to reinforce respect for universal Native spirituality, as opposed to a romanticism often associated with a Native drum. She aligns hearts through song across cultures, and encourages women to have responsibility at the drum.

April is founding Director of the nonprofit corporation Resources for Indian Student Education (RISE) in Alturas, Modoc County, California. She has been presented with the 2009 Flying Eagle Woman Community Based Philanthropy Award because of her humanitarian efforts, and promotion of Indigenous rights and culture in her community and nationwide.

Rabbi Lynn Gottlieb is a feminist peace activist and one of the first eight women to serve as a rabbi beginning in September 1973. Rabbi Lynn co-directs Middle East Programming at AFSC in San Francisco, serves as rabbi to the Danforth Jewish Circle in Toronto and is program director of Interfaith Inventions wilderness peace camps. She is a storyteller and author of the groundbreaking book, *She Who Dwells Within: A Feminist Vision of a Renewed Judaism* (1995). She co-founded the Community of Living Traditions at Stonypoint as well as Shomer Shalom Network for Jewish Nonviolence.

Judy Grahn, Ph.D., cultural theorist, poet, and activist is Co-Director & Core Faculty, Women's Spirituality MA Program, Institute of Transpersonal Psychology, Palo Alto, CA. Judy won the 2009 Lambda Literary Award in the category of Lesbian Poetry for her volume *love belongs to those who do the feeling*, which contains writing from her entire body of poetry over 40 years, from her groundbreaking *The Work of a Common Woman* to new poems written between 1997 and 2008. She also won the Lambda Literary Award in the category of Lesbian Nonfiction (1989.)

Judy authored *Blood, Bread, and Roses* (1993) and *Another Mother Tongue: Gay Words, Gay Worlds*, as well as *Queen of Swords, Queen of Wands, The Highest Apple* and many volumes of poetry; one of her famous poems, "Detroit Annie" was adapted and recorded by singer Ani DeFranco at Carnegie Hall. Judy is the Editor of Metaformia: A Journal of Menstruation and Culture (www.metaformia.org.) She is adjunct professor in the Creative Inquiry MFA Program at California Institute of Integral Studies in San Francisco. A new collection of prose and poetry, *The Judy Grahn Reader*, has been published by Aunt Lute Press. Judy's work has won an NEA Grant, an American Book Award, an American Library Award; a Lifetime Achievement Award (in Lesbian Letters), and a Founding Foremothers of Women's

Spirituality Award. Triangle Publishers feature a "Judy Grahn Non-fiction Award."

D'vorah (Deborah) J. Grenn, Ph.D., is Founder & Director, The Lilith Institute, A Center for the Study of Sacred Text, Myth & Ritual (1997); Founding Kohenet/Priestess, Mishkan Shekhinah (www.mishkanshekhinah.org) and Co-Director and Core Faculty in the Women's Spirituality M.A. Program at the Institute of Transpersonal Psychology, Palo Alto, California. D'vorah carries on her heritage by living the nomadic lifestyle of her ancestors, splitting her time between Napa and other parts of the greater San Francisco Bay Area. She was a founding Advisory Board member of the Kohenet Priestess Training Institute and is an advocate against intimate, and all forms of violence. She co-edits Metaformia: A Journal of Menstruation and Culture (www.metaformia.org) and can be reached by writing to idvorah@gmail.com.

Diane "Sollitaire" H. is a wife, mother, graduate student, anthropologist, designer, photographer, musician, blogger, writer, poet, and pagan practitioner.

Donna Henes is an internationally renowned urban shaman, eco-ceremonialist, ritual expert, spiritual counselor, award-winning author, popular speaker and workshop leader, whose joyful celebrations of celestial events have introduced ancient traditional rituals and contemporary ceremonies to millions of people in more than

100 cities since 1972. Mama Donna, as she is affectionately known, is the author of *The Queen of My Self* (about turning midlife crisis into crowning achievement,) *The Moon Watcher's Companion, Celestially Auspicious Occasions: Seasons, Cycles, and Celebrations, Dressing Our Wounds In Warm Clothes* and the CD, Reverence To Her: Mythology, the Matriarchy, & Me. She writes a syndicated column for UPI Religion and Spirituality Forum and published a monthly Ezine, The Queen's Chronicles.

In addition to teaching and lecturing worldwide, Mama Donna maintains a ceremonial center, spirit shop, ritual practice and consultancy in Exotic Brooklyn, New York, Mama Donna's Tea Garden & Healing Haven, where she works with individuals and groups to create personally relevant rituals for all of life's transitions (www.Donna-Henes.net.)

Catherine Herrera is an independent media maker, artist and writer now living with her family in San Francisco. Catherine began her career as a documentary producer and photojournalist living in Mexico City for seven years after receiving a Fulbright Fellowship. Catherine draws from her experiences and cultural heritage to create works that speak in a universal way to audiences. Catherine Herrera is the principal force behind Flor de Miel Films, which produces media programming to entertain, empower and enlighten audiences on the subjects of our time.

jme* ismyn is a Kohenet/priestess, singer/songwriter, musician and liturgist, and is founder of the Temple of the Hebrew Goddess/ Mishkan Elat (www.jamieisman.com.)

Dianne E. Jenett, Ph.D., is Co-Director & Core Faculty, Women's Spirituality M.A. Program, the Institute of Transpersonal Psychology, Palo Alto, CA. She is one of four co-authors of the qualitative research methodology, organic inquiry, first published in *Organic Inquiry: If Research Were Sacred*. Co-founder with Judy Grahn of Serpentina, a collaboration in support of Women-Centered Research for Everybody (www.serpentina.com.) Dianne's love for Kerala, India takes her there almost every year where she researches and participates in community rituals to Bhadrakali.

Her research has been published in the U.S., Europe and India; she has published "A Million Shaktis Rising: Pongala, a Woman's Festival in Kerala, India" in Journal of Feminist Studies in Religion, 21, no. 1 (2005), http://muse.jhu.edu/journals/journal_of_feminist_studies_ in_religion/v021/21.1jenett.pdf and "Menstruating Women/Menstruating Goddesses: Sites of Sacred Power in Kerala, South India, Sangam Era (100-500 CE) to the Present" In *Menstruation: History and Culture from Antiquity to Modernity*, ed. Andrew Shail, Houndmills, England: Palgrave Macmillan Ltd. – available at Metaformia journal (http://www.metaformia.org/article_09.cfm.)

Dianne also received the 2008 Community Engagement Award from the Institute of Transpersonal Psychology for her work in bringing the ideas from women's spirituality into communities beyond academia.

J'annine Jobling is Associate Professor at Liverpool Hope University, UK. Her interests focus on religious/spiritual themes in literary texts, particularly within the theoretical contexts of feminism and postmodernism. Her books include *Fantastic Spiritualities: Monsters, Heroes and the Contemporary Religious Imagination* (Continuum, forthcoming 2010), *Women and the Divine: Touching Transcendence* (co-edited with Gillian Howie; Palgrave Macmillan, 2008), and *Feminist Biblical Interpretation of the Bible* (Ashgate, 2002).

Nané Ariadne Jordan is a Ph.D. candidate, Centre for Cross-Faculty Inquiry, University of British Columbia; M.A., Women's Spirituality, New College of California; B.F.A., University of Ottawa. Nané is an artist, mother, scholar, and popular educator in the women's movement, having a background in lay midwifery. She has worked attending home births and doing post-partum care for women, their babies and families. She facilitates rites of passage rituals for birthing women, and collaborated for many years in planning the Women's Spirituality Celebration event in Vancouver, B.C. She continues to develop her ecofeminist art practice in performance ritual, video and textile art. Her current scholarly research inquires into the lived experiences and wisdom ways of women who have been students or faculty within the Women's Spirituality graduate degree program now housed at the Institute of Transpersonal Psychology, Palo Alto, California.

Malgorzata "saraswati" Kruszewska teaches Comparative Mythology and Religious Studies. Born in Poland, reborn in India, she now lives near the Russian River.

DeAnna L'Am, author of *Becoming Peers—Mentoring Girls into Womanhood*, has been teaching in the United States and internationally since 1980 in the fields of team building, conflict resolution, peacemaking, and women's spirituality. DeAnna was the first to bring Rites Of Passage work to mixed groups of Jewish & Palestinian women in Israel/Palestine, her country of origin. Her work helped participants surpass religious and political divides by deeply bonding as cycling women. Since founding Red Moon—Cycles of Women's Wisdom™ in 1994, DeAnna has been holding regular classes for mothers & daughters, for women, and for adolescent girls. DeAnna works to cultivate Red Tents in every neighborhood, and trains women to facilitate Red Tent circles. She travels to teach locally and globally; anywhere women are thirsty for this work. For more information go to: www.deannalam.com.

K.A. Laity holds a Ph.D. in Medieval Studies. Author of Pelzmantel: A Medieval Tale and other stories, she teaches medieval literature, creative writing, film and popular culture at the College of Saint Rose. Website: www.kalaity.com.

Qadesha D'vora K'lilah (Deborah Apple) was the first female to read from the Torah as Bat Mitzvah in her childhood synagogue in San Francisco. She was ordained as a minister with Heartsong in

1984, and as Kohenet in 2009, with Rabbi Jill Hammer and Holly Taya Shere. She leads Rosh Chodesh celebrations with a focus on the worship of Asherah, as well as other ancient Judaic and Ancient Near Eastern practices of embodied spirituality (www.shuvtamid.org.)

Judith Laura is the author of *She Lives! The Return of Our Great Mother* (1989, 1999), *Goddess Spirituality for the 21st Century* (1997, 2008), and two novels, the most recent of which, *Beyond All Desiring* (2005), won several awards. Her first rituals appeared in the journal Woman Spirit in 1978. Her column, "Thealogical Musings" appeared in The Beltane Papers from 2002-2007. Other of her Goddess writings have appeared inSageWoman, Matrifocus, Goddess Pages, and in anthologies. Her poetry has been widely published in journals and anthologies. She is founder and listowner of the Yahoo group, Asherah, which focuses on heritage of the divine as female in Judaism. She has a website at judithlaura.com and blogs as Medusa on medusacoils.blogspot.com.

Andrea Epel Lieberstein, MPH, RD leads women's circles, retreats and is writing a novel on the Goddess. She has been developing, teaching and coordinating mind body programs in Kaiser Permanente Northern California since 1990. Andrea specializes in helping people transform their lives through mindfulness training, stress management, nutrition and lifestyle change. She teaches mindfulness, mind body medicine, meditation, movement programs and is a stress management and wellness coach. She is committed to bringing the beauty and knowledge of the Goddess to women and men through circles, retreats, her writing and her work in the world to achieve balance with self and nature.

Xochipala Maes Valdez is a graphic artist, website designer, avid researcher, and writer. She is on faculty at The School of Ancient Mysteries/Sacred Arts Center and has lectured at universities and conferences around the world on the philosophy and theology of the sacred Ifa scriptures. Xochipala has been an initiated priest and diviner in the Futunmiṣe lineage of Ile Ife Nigeria, since 1993.

Beth Marshall holds an M.A. in Women's Spirituality and is a poet and writer. Since retiring, Beth has been trying to identify the elements of a serene and satisfying way of life for her late years. She is finding this needs to include the spiritual and the practical (meditating and making bread), physical and mental activity (yoga and poetry writing), as well as ritual and beauty (tea ceremony and dulcimer playing). Beth enjoys spending time alone and with her partner of 46 years, but also tries to stay active socially and politically, marching in her local Pride parade and leading discussions on education issues. "There are endless ways to design a fulfilling life around whatever difficulties arise in old age."

Reverend Shiloh Sophia McCloud, Minister of Sacred Arts has dedicated her adult life to the study and practice of art as a spiritual discipline as well as to helping equip women with the tools and understanding to develop their own creative potential. She has owned art galleries representing her work and the work of dozens of women artists for over ten years. Her sacred artwork provides healing images and inspirational content about women and family.

Shiloh lives and teaches a philosophy that all art forms are tools for individual, social and spiritual transformation. Shiloh teaches workshops in Northern California and online, and she is the founder of Cosmic Cowgirls Ink, LLC a woman and girl owned publishing company. She has published five books and has her cards and artwork represented in galleries and shops across the country. Shiloh is Adjunct Faculty in M.A., Women's Spirituality at the Institute of Transpersonal Psychology, Palo Alto, California, and has been happily married for over 15 years to Isaiah McCloud, a visionary musician. Websites: www.shilohsophia.com and www.cosmiccowgirls.com.

Betty De Shong Meador, Ph.D., is a Jungian analyst, retired, member and past president of the C.G. Jung Institute of San Francisco. Her translations of Sumerian myth and poetry, including all the known works of the Sumerian High Priestess Enheduanna, the first author of record, 2300 BCE, appear in her books *Uncursing the Dark, Inanna— Lady of Largest Heart*, and *Princess, Priestess, Poet—the Sumerian Temple Hymns of Enheduanna.*

Aurora Medina holds Masters degrees in both Transpersonal Psychology and Women's Spirituality. She is a social entrepreneur using the radio waves to make social change in the Hispanic community. Aurora has a Spanish radio show, "Efecto Mariposa" (Butterfly Effect) on two radio stations in the San Francisco Bay Area. The show focuses on guiding Latin women to empowerment and self-esteem. She also leads workshops and writes freelance articles on the subject of exploring women's inner strength.

Aurora specializes in the psychology of money, and is a certified money coach inspiring women to have transform their relationship with money. Part of her mission is to support other women as they strive to understand themselves in order to reach their full potential using transpersonal integration: mind, body and spirit. In her classes she incorporates visual arts, movement, ritual and the analytical mind.

Mary Beth Moser holds a Masters Degree in Women's Spirituality from New College of California and is currently a Ph.D. candidate at California Institute of Integral Studies in San Francisco. She is the author of *Honoring Darkness: Exploring the Power of Black Madonnas in Italy* (2008) and "Hidden No More: The Black Madonna Adonai of Sicily" in She Is Everywhere!—an anthology of writing in womanist/ feminist spirituality (Lucia Birnbaum, ed., 2005). Mary Beth is the founder of Dea Madre, A Black Madonna Resource Center; see http://deamadre.home.comcast.net.

Mmatshilo Motsei started her career as a nurse and midwife at in the Limpopo province, South Africa, and moved on to become a nursing lecturer, social science researcher (Wits University) and a psychology graduate (UNISA). She founded Agisanang Domestic Abuse Prevention and Training (ADAPT), an organisation using holistic healing methods to address violence against women in townships and rural villages. During her tenure as founder and director, she developed a community empowerment model for addressing domestic violence.

In her first book, *Hearing Visions, Seeing Voices*, Mmatshilo negotiates a tension-ridden life path bounded by foreign and indigenous worldviews. Her second book, *Kanga and the kangaroo court: Reflections on the rape trial of Jacob Zuma*, Mmatshilo opens the contentious issue of rape and religion with a specific focus on rape in the bible. She co-produced a documentary film, "A crack runs through it," on Afrikan people's disconnection to their spiritual roots. She won the Fair Lady White Ribbon Award for making a difference in the area of violence against women in South Africa, and was a Finalist for the South African Woman of the Year Award, Arts, culture and communications category. Mmatshilo is Managing Director of Waterdown Health Farm, an integrative health and healing facility which offers ways to integrate Afrikan spirituality, art, traditional healing and other forms of medicine to find innovative ways of healing at individual and collective levels. Info: mmatshi@mweb.co.za.

Una Nakamura is a sacred musician, music healer and member, Sisters of the Sound Continuum (SIS).

Vicki Noble, M.A. is a healer, artist, writer, and wisdom teacher, co-creator with Karen Vogel of the round feminist Motherpeace cards and author of numerous books including *Shakti Woman: Feeling Our*

Fire, Healing Our World (1991) and *The Double Goddess: Women Sharing Power* (2003). She travels and teaches internationally, including as adjunct professor in the Women's Spirituality Masters Program at the Institute of Transpersonal Psychology, Palo Alto. At home in Santa Cruz, California, she is a professional astrologer as well as an active mother, grandmother, and gardener.

Ohen Imene Nosokpikan (Nedra Williams) is a poet, visual artist, educator, Edo priestess of the West African ocean deity Olokun for 24 years and Egungun priestess. Founder of Conjure Collage Art & Design, she finds that "ancient, yet contemporary, spirituality is reflected in the design and pattern used in the creation of everyday objects, all intended to honor God on a daily basis with reverence."

A world traveler whose inspiration comes from West Africa, Morocco, India, China and the Americas, Ohen's life is heavily influenced by the aesthetic and spirituality of the African Diaspora. "That choice is neither limiting nor exclusive. The works of Romare Bearden, John Biggers, M. Ayodele, Kandinsky, Kline, Freda Kahlo and Ellen Blakely all provide inspiration. My passion, my art, exhibits a reclamation and illumination of the ancient symbols, which portray the rituals and stories of our collective remembrance."

Rabbi Leah Novick is a West Coast teacher of Jewish mysticism whose research and writing is focused on the Divine Feminine within Judaism. Leah is the author of *On the Wings of Shekhinah: Rediscovering Judaism's Divine Feminine* (Quest Books 2008) and producer of a CD of guided meditations on the same theme. She has also written biographies of Jewish women saints which were integrated into a theatre piece.

Rabbi Leah has provided rabbinical leadership to both alternative and conventional Jewish groups. She has been honored as "Pathfinder" by the Aleph Alliance for Jewish Renewal in recognition of her pioneering work in bringing the feminine into contemporary Jewish liturgy and rituals. She is featured in the International Hadassah calendar of "Women Rabbis around the World" and cited in numerous books and periodicals.

Amana Oh, Ph.D., Integral Studies, wrote her dissertation, *Cosmogonical Worldview in Jomon Pottery*, on the worldview of an ancient prehistoric Japanese culture, the Jomon culture. She analyzed the decoration of a specific type of pottery—which has a human face—whose figure resembles the female body. Her work presents an interpretation of the abstract meaning of the number three as a symbolic representation of the creation of life, bringing attention to the invisible divine energy at the core.

Amana is a spiritual healer, offering private and group sessions using her multi-dimensional energywork skills (www.luminaconnections.com.) She helps people empower themselves by guiding them to connect with their own divine Self. Her lifework is to bring deeper understandings of contemporary issues of sexism and racism from the perspective of an ancient wisdom and spirituality. She describes herself as a "Japanese Korean in California."

Alicia Ostriker, a poet and critic, has been nominated twice for a National Book Award. She is author of eleven volumes of poetry, including *No Heaven* (2005) and *the volcano sequence* (2002.) Her most recent volume of poetry criticism is *Dancing at the Devil's Party: Essays on Poetry, Politics, and the Erotic*. Her poetry has appeared in The New Yorker, American Poetry Review, The Atlantic, Paris Review, Ontario Review, The Nation, and many other journals and anthologies. She has also published *Feminist Revision and the Bible*, the controversial *The Nakedness of the Fathers: Biblical Visions and Revisions*, a combination of prose and poetry that re-imagines the Bible from the perspective of a contemporary Jewish woman, and *For the Love of God; the Bible as an Open Book*, essays on the Song of Songs, Ruth, Psalms, Ecclesiastes, Jonah and Job.

Alicia has received awards from the National Endowment for the Arts, the Poetry Society of America, the Rockefeller Foundation, and the Guggenheim Foundation. She lives in Princeton, New Jersey with her husband and is Professor Emerita of English at Rutgers University and is faculty in Drew University's Low-Residency Poetry MFA Program.

Louise Pare holds a Ph.D. in Women's Spirituality and is Director of Religious Education, Rogue Valley Unitarian Universalist Fellowship. Movement and healing arts educator and ritualist who work is informed by training in Transformational Movement, Authentic Movement and Continuum.

Silvia Parra (MamaCoAtl) earned her M.A. degree in Women's Spirituality, Performance Activism, Creative Inquiry MFA, Reiki Master, Absolute Balance Mastery ™ practitioner, Songstress, Poet, Mother, community organizer, ARTivist. She comes from the Shamanic traditions of The Curandera and syncretizes her talents and paths of wisdom to explore the dynamics of emancipation as as power source for public health. Focused on the work of Women and the recovery of the Indigenous Soul, she has organized public ceremonies to heal the waters of the river Mother of God in the Amazon where she studied with Ayahuasca healers of Peru, Brazil, and Bolivia. In Mexico she has curated healing ceremonies for public spaces where the bodies of murdered women have been found. She periodically puts together public healings called Limpias in her beloved Mission District in San Francisco and is actively involved in the arts. Her website can be found at: www.myspace.com/mamacoatl.

Pennie Opal Plant is a daughter, sister, aunt, mother and grandmother who has been writing since childhood. She is of Yaqui, Mexican, Cherokee, Choctaw, Algonquin and European descent. She has a big, loud laugh which she tries to use as often as possible. An activist on behalf of life, Mother Earth & Native American concerns since 1981, she has worked on issues regarding the environment, uranium mining, Native America, nuclear weapons, and the release of political prisoner Leonard Peltier.

She has been heard saying "if it isn't fun, I don't want to play" and "if you don't learn to share, you will wind up with nothing". She has been a small business owner since 1985. Since 1991, she has owned a Native American gallery, Gathering Tribes, in Albany, California. She is active in the San Francisco Bay Area Native American community and is currently writing a children's book which will be illustrated by her partner, Michael Horse, a Native American artist, jeweler and actor. While she doesn't enjoy juggling, she has become a master at plate spinning...a plate of activism here, a plate of business there, a plate of family here, a plate of laughter there.

Evelie Delfino Sáles Posch is a sacred song singer/writer; recording artist; drummer; dancer; Tibetan and Kundalini yogini; healer; choral director; storyteller; actress; music educator; independent scholar and magical activist whose talents have flourished for over forty years, spanning the traditions of her ancestors and the progressive edge of ceremony, world music and dance. Recognized as a Babaylan (Filipino healer, seer, ceremonialist) by the "father of Philippine psychology" Dr. Virgilio "Ver" Enriquez, Evelie founded "Babaylan Emerging: Apprenticeship and Mentoring (BEAM) Program" which explores the indigenous spirituality of pre-Hispanic Philippines for today's Filipina.

Evelie has sung at the Mormon Tabernacle, Lincoln Center and at Kennedy Center in Washington, D.C. She performs with/directs Mahal, a kosmik-ethnik-ekstatik-trance-tribal fusion muzik ensemble; Kismat-Mahal Kirtan Ensemble, which offers devotional music;

and the Spiral Dance Chorus and Band for Reclaiming's annual Samhain celebration. She also sings with Ya Elah; for Jennifer Berezan's "Praises for the World"; at Sophia in Trinity Saturday masses led by Roman Catholic Woman Priest Victoria Rue.

Evelie teaches Core classes for Reclaiming, and classes in chanting, drumming, ritual magic, movement and dance throughout the San Francisco Bay Area. She facilitates satsangs, meditations, and creative workshops, and is currently a Bard of Taliesin (Order of Bards, Ovates and Druids out of Great Britain) and Master, Bardic Arts for the first Gorsedd (gathering) of Druids. She has co-led Techno Cosmic Masses and has sung for the mayors of San Francisco and Oakland of the past 16 years. Guest faculty, Women's Spirituality MA Program, CIIS, Dominican University, Center for the Divine Feminine/Women's Spirituality Program at Institute of Transpersonal Psychology, and Holy Names College.

Tina Proctor earned an MS in wildlife biology from Colorado State University which led to a career with several agencies including 17 years with the U.S. Fish and Wildlife Service. This work deepened her lifelong love of the natural world. Her second passion has been teaching goddess history, myth and ritual to women for the past 12 years. She completed an MA in Women's Spirituality at New College of California in 2006 (a program which has since moved to the Institute of Transpersonal Psychology in Palo Alto, CA.) Her paper, "Women, Orangutans and the Moon," combined her two passions and was published in the on-line journal, Metaformia: A Journal of Menstruation and Culture.

Tina's book for middle-school girls, *Ophelia's Oracle* (2009) co-authored with Donna DeNomme, is the first of a girl's motivational series. Through exercises and stories of real girls who embody goddess qualities, it tells the story of a pre-teen, Ophelia, who hears about the Divine Feminine through goddess stories from her grandmothers and other women. She explores her feelings about what it means to be a teenage girl today, and in the end, the stories lead her to embrace her own female intuitive wisdom. Tina writes, tells stories, and creates ceremonies for females of all ages. She and her husband, Dennis Grogan, have led a Peace Circle for eight years and are trained labyrinth facilitators.

Lauren Raine, MFA is a visionary artist, ritualist, choreographer and mask artist. Lauren has published *The Masks of the Goddess: Sacred Masks & Dance* and *Spider Woman's Hands: Weaving a New Web*. After studying traditions of "Temple masks" in Bali, Lauren produced collaborative masks with Balinese mask artists including Ida Bagus Anom which were exhibited at Buka Creati Gallery in Ubud, Bali. Returning to the U.S., she made 35 multi-cultural masks of Goddesses for The 20th Annual Spiral Dance at Ft. Mason Center in San Francisco. The collection traveled throughout the U.S. for 7 years, at venues such as the University of Creation Spirituality in Oakland, the Chapel of the Sacred Mirrors in NYC and the Muse Community Arts Center in Tucson.

Lauren offers workshops that explore mythology and mask making, and has taught at the Kripalu Institute, Lilydale Conference Center, Sedona Art Center, and elsewhere. In 2009 she will be resident artist at the Henry Luce Center for the Arts at Wesley Theological Seminary in Washington, D.C.

Rabbi Geela Rayzel Raphael, a Reconstructionist/Renewal rabbi, and singer/songwriter, is a liturgist and innovative ritualist. Geela is Rabbinic Director of the Interfaith Family Support Network in Philadelphia and of the Jewish Creativity Project. See her website at http://www.shechinah.com/grr/rabbi.html.

Arisika Razak, RN, CNM (Certified Nurse Midwife), MPH (Masters in Public Health) is Director, Women's Spirituality M.A. and Ph.D. programs in Philosophy and Religion at California Institute of Integral Studies, San Francisco. She has worked for over thirty years integrating the teachings of earth-based spiritual traditions, women's spirituality, and women's health into the language of movement and dance.

Arisika has articles in *Children of the Dawn: Visions of the New Family; Reweaving the World: the Emergence of Eco-feminism,* and wrote the introduction to *Childbirth Wisdom.* In Fire Eyes, the full-length feature film by an African woman to discuss the issue of female circumcision, Arisika discusses her work with women and their bodies, as a midwife and healer. She is also interviewed in Abortion: From Danger to Dignity, by Academy Award nominee, Dorothy Fadiman, and in the PBS documentary Who Lives, Who Dies?, on issues of health care for the indigent.

Arisika has led workshops at universities throughout Northern California. She is the featured dancer in A Place of Rage by Prahtibha Parma which showcases the work of African-American women activists Alice Walker, June Jordan and Angela Davis.

As an artist performer, Arisika's work is dedicated to the reclamation of the power and sacredness of the female body. Arisika has performed professionally since 1987, appearing at over 75 venues, including the Fourth UN Conference on the Status of Women in Beijing, China, the Women of Wisdom, Women of Power Conference in Bern Switzerland; the Michigan Women's Music Festival in Michigan, Stanford University, Theatre Artaud, La Pena Community Center, and the University of Southern California Ecofeminist Conference in Los Angeles. She has been a core member of the Purple Moon Dance Project for over four years.

Julianne Reidy has an M.A. in Women's Spirituality, New College of California; M.F.A., Creative Inquiry, California Institute of Integral Studies. Consummate Researcher and Librarian.

Pauline Reif has her M.A. in Women's Spirituality from the Institute of Transpersonal Psychology in Palo Alto, California. She is a poet, teacher and interfaith chaplain, facilitating workshops exploring the

Sacred Feminine and guest lectures on the same. Her poems have appeared in various literary journals. She lives in the San Francisco Bay Area near her grandchildren.

Patricia Lynn Reilly, M. Div. is a publishing coach and creativity consultant known for her inspirational books, resources, and the poem, "Imagine A Woman." Patricia's poem is excerpted with kind permission from A God Who Looks Like Me (Ballantine Books,1995) and Imagine a Woman in Love with Herself (Conari Press, 1999). For more about her creative agency and writings, visit http:// www.OpenWindowCreations.com. Patricia lives in western Michigan and loves her walks along Lake Michigan.

Kaye Schuman, sculptor, painter and avid reader, is a vibrant intellectual and Renaissance person who writes "for my own amusement and amazement... I've sculpted and painted purely for my own pleasure." Kaye loves literature and the Yiddish language, and used to write poetry in Yiddish. She is passionate about her cultural Judaism.

Maya Spector is a children's librarian, storyteller, poet, ritualist, and certified SoulCollage facilitator. She is a regular presenter at Bay Area oral traditions events such as The Great Night or Rumi. Maya is proud to be a member of Stone Dancers, a women's circle meeting weekly since 1984. More of her work may be found at: www.barryandmayaspector.com.

Cheryl Straffon is a writer of books on the Goddess, including *The Earth Goddess* (1998) & *Daughters of the Earth* (2007). She also edits Goddess Alive! magazine (See website at http://www.goddess alive.co.uk/) and co-facilitates Goddess Tours International (www.goddess-tours-international.com). She lives with her partner and 2 cats for most of the year in Cornwall, Britain, but also has a home in Crete. She has celebrated the Celtic 8 festivals of the Wheel of the Year for about 30 years now, without missing one, and particularly loves Imbolc and the annual re-emergence of Brigid into consciousness.

Chief Luisah Teish is Founder and President of Ile Orunmila Oshun (the House of Destiny and Love.) She holds a chieftancy title from the Fatunmiṣe compound in Ile Ife, Nigeria, and is also an Iyanifa (Mother of Destiny.) Teish is a writer, storyteller and creative projects consultant, as well as founder of the School of Ancient Mysteries/Sacred Arts Center in Oakland, California. Her writings include *Jambalaya, The Natural Woman's Book of Personal Charms and Practical Rituals* (1988), *Carnival of the Spirits, Jump Up!* and the booklet "Women, Look Deep" co-authored with Leilani Birely and Deborah Grenn. Presently she is developing curricula to address issues of ecology, spirituality, environmental justice and art. For information about Teish's classes, rituals events and services, see luisahteish.com and/or www.ileorunmilaoshun.org.

Charlie Toledo is of Towa descendant, native to New Mexico. She is the Executive Director of the Suscol Intertribal Council, a community-based non-profit organization in Napa, California, incorporated in 1992. She also has been in private practice as a certified masseuse, certified hypnotherapist and meditation teacher since 1982. She has extensive experience as public speaker, presenter and community organizer in regional, statewide, national and international forums. She has been an organic gardener since 1978. She has a lifelong commitment to social justice and international work on Human Rights.

Charlie has been very active in furthering cross-cultural exchange with Pomo and Maori (New Zealand) as well as Ecuadorian women, as well as helping to bring attention to the struggles of women of Afghanistan and Uganda. She served as California Women's Action Agenda (CAWA) Napa County chair; as Suscol Council representative to the Napa Valley Alliance for Arts and Culture; as Chair of the Women's Intercultural Network (WIN), and as Suscol representative on the Coalition of Native American Associations and California Rural Indian Health Board program. For more about her work, see the website http://suscol.nativeweb.org.

Rashidah Tutashinda is a daughter of Oya, Orisha Goddess of Change, and Ph.D. student, Women's Spirituality at the California Institute of Integral Studies, San Francisco.

Elka Eastly Vera has her B.A. in Literature. She is a Reclaiming tradition priestess and teacher; Reiki master/teacher; certified clinical hypnotherapist, transformational facilitator and communication arts consultant.

Karen Nelson Villanueva, M.A., M.P.A. and Ph.D. candidate in Women's Spirituality, California Institute of Integral Studies, San Francisco. Essays have included "For the Love of Us All: The Black Madonna as a Symbol of Peace and Refuge from Fear" and "Mother Love in Buddhism," published in the Journal for the Association for Research on Mothering. Karen is one of the editors of She is Everywhere! Volume II: An anthology of writings in womanist/feminist spirituality, Authors Choice Press, 2008.

Kate Wolf-Pizor is an Elder Celtic priestess in the Gardnerian tradition. She is also a Senior Clinical faculty member at the Institute of Transpersonal Psychology in Palo Alto, California where she teaches clinical classes, teaches Wicca, and leads ritual whenever she can. She is a licensed Marriage and Family Therapist and has a private practice in Mountain View, California.

Lady Wren was first ordained as a priestess in the Wiccan tradition in the mid-eighties in Monterey, California. Wren says she was a misfit most of her life, and only realized in her forties that she was a witch. In 1990, she moved from Monterey to Key West, and trained in the Gardnerian tradition for five years, moving up to 2nd degree, but declining 3rd degree. Always restless, she moved again to Las Vegas and joined the Desert Moon Circle where she was elevated to High Priestess under Lady Katlyn. Another move brought Wren to Santa

Rosa, California in 1999, where she co-founded another group that met regularly to celebrate Solstices, Equinoxes and other holidays on the Wheel of the Year.

Wren recently relocated to Hawaii, and now circles with an established group in Honolulu. "I have no doubt that I am 'Wiccan to the bone'—to quote one of my apprentices—and that this is just one more life in a line of many spent delving into the mysteries, and honoring the Goddess and her consort." Known as Wren, the rune lady, she is an artisan dealing in magickal tools as well as divination sets, and has been teaching the runic mysteries since 1996. "My work is a reflection of my path, as I engrave runes and other mystical symbols. I have felt the guiding hand of the Goddess in my work and my life, and am honored to represent her in circle, blessed with her inspiration. The Goddess has given me a livelihood which is in harmony with my spirit. Blessed be."

Additional Credits

TEXT

With thanks to all for their kind permissions to include these works in this volume:

Judy Grahn's "may we embrace" - copyright by the author May 2003 - All Rights Reserved. Originally published by Serpentina Publications, and recently published in her book *love is for those who do the feeling* by Red Hen Press (2008). Available soon on Lunarchy's forthcoming CD. Her poem "Dancing in Place" was originally published in *Queen of Swords*.

Betty De Shong Meador's piece is excerpted from her forthcoming essay in *Goddesses in World Religion*, Patricia Monaghan, ed. (Praeger/Greenwood, 2010).

D'vorah J. Grenn's Invocation to Inanna-Lilith-Shekhinah was first delivered at the "Divina et Femina" conference at University of Ottawa, 2000. Reprinted from *The Masks of the Goddess* (Lauren Raine, 2008).

Luisah Teish's poems are from *Jambalaya: The Natural Woman's Book of Personal Charms and Practical Rituals* (HarperSanFrancisco, 1988) and her earlier work, "She Who Whispers" (1983).

Alicia Ostriker's poem *the shekhinah as mute*, is from the volcano sequence, University of Pittsburgh Press, 2002.

Uzuri Amini's prayer was originally published in *The Goddess Celebrates*, Diane Stein, ed. (Crossing Press, 1991)

Mariam Baker's prayer is excerpted from her forthcoming book, *A SACRED VOICE, Stories of Women and Islam.*

Patricia Lynn Reilly's piece is From her *Prayers, Blessings, and Invocations to the Divine Feminine, 1996-1999.*

Andrea Epel Lieberstein's contribution is excerpted from her forthcoming novel *Goddess Awakening.*

Alisa Fineman's lyrics reprinted from her CD *Closing the Distance*, 2004.

Cheryl Dawson's story is an excerpt from her forthcoming essay "Divine Conversation."

Mmatshilo Motsei's "Prayer for Afrika" is taken from her forthcoming poetry compilation, *Moondance.*

Laura Amazzone's piece on Durga and Nepal is excerpted from her forthcoming book *Durga: Empowering Women, Transforming the World,* to be published by Hamilton Books, an imprint of University Books, 2010.

Judith Laura's "Prayer to Mother Earth" originally appeared in the 10th Anniversary Edition [1999] of *She Lives! The Return of Our Great Mother* as "Earth Invocation." It is reprinted here by permission of the author.

Nané Ariadne Jordan wrote "To the Earth and Birth Goddess" and "The snake, the tree" as invocations to Goddess within her Master's thesis in Women's Spirituality, New College of California, San Francisco, CA—*Earthdance, Birthdance: The Power and Passion of Women Giving Birth, a pilgrim's path to birth.*

D'vorah J. Grenn's "A Celebration of Her, and of Life" was originally written for the Mishkan Shekhinah siddur/prayerbook in 2007.

ART

Gratitude to Chief Fajembola Fatunmiṣe, Luisah Teish for allowing us to publish her original drawing "As the Sea Sees," and to Dr. Rita Casey for giving permission to reprint one of the Sumerian pictographs she has brought to light and life. "Dwelling Place of the Divine," the pictograph which opens and closes this book, is taken from a Sumerian clay tablet symbol c. 4500 BCE, and is representative of the pictographs expressed in Mesopotamian stories and hymns. Thanks, too, to independent scholar and artist Max Dashu, for her "Amulet of Allat" artwork.

The Tanit sketches on the following page are from Il tempio a pozzo di Santa Cristina by Professor Franco Laner, Guida2 Edizioni Adrastea, 2004. Courtesy of www.archeotour.eu.

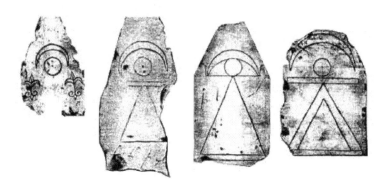